ASTROSHAM

book 1

A Journey into the Inner Universe

Franco Santoro

FINDHORN
Press

First published in 2003

ISBN 1-84409-009-4

British Library Cataloguing-in-Publication Data.
A catalogue record for this book is available from the British Library.

Edited by Lynn Barton
Layout by Pam Bochel
Cover design by Thierry Bogliolo
Cover photograph © PhotoDisc
Illustrations © Franco Santoro

Printed and bound by WS Bookwell, Finland

Published by

Findhorn Press

305a The Park, Findhorn
Forres IV36 3TE
Scotland
Tel 01309 690582
Fax 01309 690036
e-mail: info@findhornpress.com
findhornpress.com

Contents

FOREWORD

This is a wonderful book. Franco has published an earlier version of this book in Italian, but readers of the English version are privileged to get an expanded edition of the earlier Italian work.

I first read Franco's writing when he began translating some of the introductory material and the chapters on the Twelve Sectors from the Italian into English. A group of us at Findhorn were doing the first year of the training offered by Franco. As we met each month Franco would give us the literature for the relevant sector. At the beginning I could only manage to read a couple of paragraphs at a time, so overwhelming was the combination of depth and detail that Franco conveys.

Franco always stresses the overriding importance of experiential work and the value of information from our own journeys rather than from the written word. Yet I also recall him saying that when our minds have been provided with adequate explanations and had some of their questions answered, then barriers can come down and fears can be released, with a beneficial result in terms of being able to open up to and trust those non-ordinary experiences.

Initially Franco was reluctant to translate any of this material, but over time and with a massive amount of work, the present expanded and updated book has emerged. My heartfelt thanks to him.

Judy Wyld
July 2002

PREFACE

This work is the attempt to bring light into the apparent darkness of the ancient origins of a wonderful remembrance, so as to allow the emergence of what has for long been there, undisturbed, in an oasis of velvet and dark clouds. Its aim is to acknowledge the reality of that remembrance, awaken its energy, establish a regular connection with it and allow its growing emanation within and without. It is a journey in the inner and outer world supported by the adherence to the INTENT and FUNCTION. The Function is the total alignment with the divine will of existence and represents the maximum achievable purpose on the human level. The Intent is the specific application of the Function: the creative contribution, apparently individual, connected to the realisation of the divine will. The Intent is to be connected to the Function.

– Ur Kraab

ACKNOWLEDGEMENTS

Part of the material incorporated in this book constitutes the translation and revision of chapters taken from my book (Franco Santoro, *Iniziazione all'astrosciamanesimo: la via zodiacale alla Guida Interiore*, Edizioni Mediterranee, Rome, 2000) previously published in Italian by Edizioni Mediterranee. Hence I deeply appreciate the publisher's permission to integrate it in this renewed and expanded work.

I wish to gratefully acknowledge the permission to use quotations from the works listed below:

Portions of *A Course in Miracles*® copyright 1975, 1992, 1996 reprinted by permission of the *Foundation for A Course in Miracles, Inc.*® (www.facim.org). All rights reserved.

Osho, *Meditation: The First and Last Freedom*, St. Martin's Press, New York, NY, 1996; *Hidden Mysteries*, Rebel Publishing House, Pune, 1997. Used by permission of the *Osho International Foundation*, (http://www.osho.com)

Edwin C. Steinbrecher, *The Inner Guide Meditation: A Spiritual Technology for the 21st Century*, Samuel Weiser, York Beach, ME, 1988. Reprinted by permission of Samuel Weiser Inc.

Mattie Davis-Wolfe and David Thomson, *Walking the Sacred Wheel: A Year's Journey of Initiation around the Sacred Wheel*, Sacred Circles Institute, Mukilteo, WA, 1995.

Michael Harner, for citations from Michael Harner, *The Way of the Shaman*, Harper, San Francisco, CA, 1990.

Inner Traditions for quotes from Belinda Gore, *Ecstatic Body Postures: An Alternate Reality Workbook*, Bear & Company, Santa Fe, NM, 1995.

Princeton University Press, for quotes from Mircea Eliade, *Shamanism: Archaic Techniques of Ecstasy*, Princeton University Press, Princeton, NJ,1972.

Maritha Pottenger, for quotes from *Encounter Astrology*, TIA Publications, Los Angeles, 1978; *Astro Essentials: Planets in Signs, Houses & Aspects*, ACS Publications, San Diego, CA, 1991.

Marcus Allen, for citation from Marcus Allen, *Astrology for the New Age: An Intuitive Approach*, CRCS Publications, Sebastopol, CA, 1979.

Jeff Jawer, for citation from Jeff Jawer, 'Astrodrama' in Joan McEvers (ed.), *Spiritual, Metaphysical and New Trends in Modern Astrology*, Llewellyn, St. Paul, MN, 1988.

ProvOrdo Etnai Pratinindhe Pradhikara's Southern Europe Archives for the Year 1984, Anaghaseva, 1985; *ProvOrdo Etnai Sagdhanatabe*, Anaghaseva, 1988. Used by dispensation of Anaghaseva.

Careful work was made to receive permission to reprint brief citations from previously published sources. In a few cases, permission was not granted in time for formal acknowledgment. Any omission will be corrected in future editions upon notification. However, all published quotations have been officially listed in the related notes and bibliography.

I would like to offer my deepest appreciation to all those who, in different ways and times, have supported and helped me in my work. In particular I am grateful to my parents Marisa Testoni and Nunzio Santoro, my sister Annamaria Santoro, Grazia Romano, all my relatives and ancestors, Cluny Hill College and its territory, the members, guests and all beings, seen and unseen, of the Findhorn Foundation and the New Findhorn Association in the north-east of Scotland, all the researchers attending astroshamanic events, workshops and individual sessions in Great Britain, Italy, Germany, Greece and other parts of the world. Abundant gratitude to my Guides and mentors, Ur Ichì, Ur Kraab, Ur Kuran, Ji N'kho, Ratusel, the Bhi Jinah, the Sacred Cone Circle, the Delegate Authority of the Provisional Order (ProvOrdo Etnai), A.F.S. Bogus, Osho, Kabir Jaffe, the Sacro Cerchio in Bologna. I wish to give special mention and appreciation to Judy Wyld who attentively went over the first draft. Loving thanks to Thierry and Karin Bogliolo at Findhorn Press for their decisive support, Lynn Barton for her precious editorial assistance and Pam Bochel for the final layout. Grateful and heartfelt acknowledgement also to Tina Agiorgiti, Leo Anfolsi, Michael Barnett, Lucia Bruno, Eileen Caddy, Gianni Canonico at Edizioni Mediterranee, Mattie Davis-Wolfe, Rita Inì, Katharina Kroeber, Fiona Mackenzie, Pumapahe, Penelope Perrin, Paola Pierpaoli, David Thomson, Sauro Tronconi, the Podere Valpisa, the authors mentioned in the bibliography and many other soul friends and companions, who I have not mentioned for lack of space or memory. To all my relationships in all times and spaces I express my deepest gratitude. *Kahesha Opa!*

The ideas expressed in this book, unless otherwise ascribed, are my own and do not necessarily agree with those of the persons, beings or institutions mentioned in these acknowledgements.

INTRODUCTION

This book is the first of two, aimed at providing a brief introduction to the principles and practices of astroshamanism. The term *astroshamanism* identifies a spiritual system of healing aimed at expanding human perception through the integration of the basic principles of shamanism with experiential astrology, the contemporary western cultures and the revival of archaic mystery traditions. Its present form is the result of researches developed since 1976, thanks to the contribution of shamans and teachers of various cultures and dimensions.

The intent of this work is to stimulate the awareness, the exploration, the acknowledgment and the retrieval of one's inner potential. As its structure is based on the circle, what is not immediately understandable will be clarified as the readers proceed with their experiences. This text is aimed at supporting the spiritual path of each individual, not at becoming a substitute for that path.

The present book introduces some of the theoretical aspects and practical tools on which astroshamanism is based. First it considers astrology and its relationship with shamanism. Then it provides details about the Sacred Circle, the concepts of Intent and Function, a series of astroshamanic basic practices and rituals, the astroshamanic voyage, the Spirit Guide, the Totem Spirits, the Spirit Medicines and Sacred Tools, and further shamanic techniques. This book ends with a brief description of some aspects of the astrological language, as it is employed in astroshamanism, and with a coda featuring a compendium of one of the basic myths to which the astroshamanic tradition refers. The second book is devoted to the exploration of the Sacred Circle and consists of sections dealing with each of its Twelve Sectors and Four Directions. Information on the characteristics and correspondences of the various energies of the Sacred Circle is provided, together with specific practices, rituals and experiential reports of astroshamanic voyages.

Astroshamanism can be applied in the context of any culture or tradition. In the way in which I have developed it, this work refers to the following basic models: the *Sacred Circle;* the work on *release,* or *forgiveness;* and the *Epic of the Sacred Cone.*

The *Sacred Circle* and its various applications – astrology included – represent the general structure of astroshamanism. Its purpose is to achieve balance, integration and unity through a process of circular learning that refers to the subtle cycles of the Earth and the universe. Each lesson and experience is repeated in different ways and from various perspectives until it is totally learned. When this occurs, a passage to a new level of perception takes place: the circle ceases to rotate along the same circumference and opens up to a spiral movement to start a new cycle of transformation.

The work on *release,* or *forgiveness,* represents the major function of astroshamanism. This is the attitude that allows me to let go of my limited identification and expand the scope of my awareness. References include here: the western mystery and hermetic traditions, basic shamanism and *A Course in Miracles.®*

The Epic of the Sacred Cone constitutes a mythic and strategic transposition of the models of the Sacred Circle and the work on release, or forgiveness. It includes information – in the form of messages, visions, rituals and practices – derived from the work with a specific shamanic lineage that I identify here with the term *Sacred Cone Circle,* or *ProvOrdo Etnai.* These teachings represent the original reference tradition of astroshamanism. Their basic intent is to foster the process of release of grievances and reawakening of our original memories through a relationship of exchange with multi-dimensional realities. In this context initiation is not about receiving outstanding powers and radically shifting my perception of life, although this at times may also happen. It is a process that involves implanting a seed, which will stimulate my potential and grow in accordance with my investment of energy and natural disposition. This development stems from the essence of all mystery traditions (*mystery* from the Greek myein, 'to keep silent', and *tradition* from the Latin tradere, 'to hand down, surrender, transmit'). The principal trait of these mysteries is that they cannot be communicated by one human being to another. Although esoteric teachers or shamans can at times provide the tools and itinerary to access basic information, the actual mysteries are revealed to the initiates only by direct experience and connection with their own multi-dimensional nature, or Spirit Guides.

The image of the *cone* includes both that of the *circle* and the *triangle*. It describes a spiral circular movement that, starting from an original emanation point, creatively develops ad infinitum. This represents the progressive demanifestation process of this universe, the ascentional movement of matter toward the reality of spirit, the abandonment of the illusion of separation created by the ego and the journey back to unity. This process does not occur by escaping or transcending the physical dimension, but through using it as a teaching device to fulfil one's true purpose in this plane of existence. The present text is a tribute to this vision.

The information given in the book covers a large amount of material. Understanding of it will depend on your level of experience, which will differ from reader to reader. Sometimes the information will be very familiar and obvious, while at other times you may find yourself unclear or overwhelmed by what is presented. Some of the ideas contained in this book could cause different reactions. You may find them hard to believe, weird, obvious, naive, startling, revealing, glamorous, absurd, fascinating, meaningful or inspiring. You do not need to believe or accept what is written. What I am trying to express relates to experiences which are not defined or symbolically represented by ordinary human languages. In this attempt I employ a limited perspective of observation and this implies that I use expressions that are understandable according to the partial visions and experiences of a human being. These are not absolute truths. They are just pieces of a puzzle that is waiting to be completed by your own experiences and visions.

Astroshamanism is based on the awareness of the existence of an ecstatic and united dimension that lies beyond the illusions of the ordinary perception of reality. The certitude that human beings, through the progressive release of their separated and grieving identities, can have unlimited access to such a dimension constitutes the experiential essence of this work.

Note on gender: To avoid the clumsiness and overemphasis of opposite polarities inherent in the use of double personal pronouns like he/she, her/him, unless I specifically refer to a female creature or goddess, I use the generic terms he, him, his to indicate human and non-ordinary beings in general, both male and female. This is a makeshift option due to the fact that in the

English language there is no appropriate singular personal pronoun that applies equally to men and women. Therefore I would like to make clear that in the context of this book the forms he, him, his are meant to be inclusive and could as well have been replaced by she, her.

CHAPTER 1

ASTROLOGY AND SHAMANISM

As above, so below. As below, so above. So that the miracle of One be accomplished. This celebrated quotation from the *Tabula smaragdina* attributed to Hermes Trismegistus[1] constitutes the essential principle of astrology. Briefly, it means that Heaven and Earth reflect each other, that whatever exists within and without, from the smallest particle to the biggest galaxy, represents the repetition of the same system. The basic assumption of astrology is that there is no separation: our inner and outer worlds are the reflection of the same whole of which we are all part. Although it is, both spiritually and scientifically, evident that the ultimate reality of the universe is the unity of each of its components, most of humankind does not seem to be aware of this experience. Human beings appear to continue and hold the conviction of existing as separate entities. The investment in this belief is so rooted and widespread as to give form to an articulated collective hallucination that reveals itself in most aspects of human life. The structure of this hallucination I denominate here as the *ego*.[2]

In a remote and unknown sphere of time and space, something occurred that caused a shift from the awareness of unity to the illusion of separation. 'Into eternity, where all is one,' says *A Course in Miracles,* 'there crept a tiny, mad idea, at which the Son of God remembered not to laugh. In his forgetting did the thought become a serious idea, and possible of both accomplishment and real effects.'[3] This mad idea is that of thinking of living as separate entities, with private histories and thoughts, whereas its *real effects* are the ego with all the grievances and fragmented forms that I perceive in the world. Yet the memory of my true nature has never abandoned me. Although hidden by thick clouds, my original Self has continued to whisper through the obscure corridors of the mind, employing all kinds of tools to remind me of my true matrix of unity. Astrology, in its purest and uncontaminated expression, had been originally conceived as a tool to remove the blocks to the perception of unity. Astrology considers the illusory situation to which humankind has relegated itself and operates *so that the miracle of One be accomplished.* In other words, as I have produced the world I see as real through the belief in separation and the identification with the ego, astrology starts from this distorted perception to gradually lead me beyond it. In the zodiacal circle each form stands in the apparent perception of most acute conflicts: male and female, day and night, life and death, Heaven and Earth, love and hate, happiness and pain, etc. Astrology features different symbols and categories that, whilst appearing separate, are inevitably part of one single unity: that of the zodiacal circle. In order to reveal to human beings the reality of unity, astrology employs the first idiom that they are able to understand: the dualistic and competitive language of the ego. This situation has caused various misunderstandings and controversies in dealing with astrology. Also the use of astrological language as a camouflage in times of severe persecution has further complicated the problem.[4]

Astrology is based on the identity of cause and effect, or subject and object. Due to this equality, its perception and interpretative structure has changed according to the prevalent cultures and spirituality of the times. In the last century, the left side of the brain, analytical and verbal, has prevailed over the intuitive and imaginative right side. Astrology, in common with other approaches, has become too abstract and theoretical and has forgotten that our original relationship with the stars was experiential and alive. Astrology includes all the universe: it is like an immense geographical map able to describe all kinds of realities. It represents, in the words of Jung, 'the summation of all the psychological knowledge of antiquity.'[5] This is extremely stimulating, but excessive attention to the map and its details has caused us to lose sight of the reason for which the map itself had been created: i.e. effectively to go on a journey. The map is not the territory, just as the menu is not the meal.

Experiential Astrology

The astrology to which I refer is an *experiential astrology*. As such it employs tools that translate the zodiacal symbols into direct experiences. The astrological chart is not interpreted or analysed, but reveals itself through emotions, movement, dance, sounds, visions and situations aimed at waking us up and connecting us with our true nature. This type of astrology represents the way back to the primeval origins of astrological language meant as a shamanic tool of communication with the forces of the universe. Its aim is to relate us to the roots of our spiritual traditions and to integrate in the current time all the heritage of knowledge from which we have separated ourselves.

The modern revival of experiential astrology dates back to the 70s. In the psychotherapeutic field, the development of alternative approaches, like the Human Potential Movement, encouraged the use of new models aimed at activating individual hidden potentials and emphasising different perspectives of evaluation. Personal responsibility in particular, rather than the victim role or the identification of the patient as patient, assumed major importance. During the same period, the rediscovery of shamanism, the resurgence of the western mystery traditions, the development of new spiritual movements and communities, the emergence of the New Age and the diffusion of eastern techniques of meditation contributed to boosting the interest in transpersonal and non-ordinary states of consciousness. In this context the tendency to trace back causes of grievances to childhood, social environment or, more esoterically, to past lives or the positions of planets became less relevant. For many advanced therapists and seekers it was not essential anymore to know the past events affecting a person, but rather to understand why certain harmful scripts or actions were repeated although there was the possibility of using different models. The transformation of such scripts and the development of inner potential became the aim of many operators. In order to support this process various tools were rediscovered and employed. Astrology was one of them. Maritha Pottenger, a pioneer in this field, expressed some of her views as follows: 'I believe strongly that getting to know our own beings and opening to growth and change is THE single most important task in our lives. I also believe that the "Truth" has many sides. I am firmly convinced there is no single ONE way to truth. Each of us must find the path uniquely his or hers. Because there are so many different ways to grow, there are many different self-help aids on the market. [...] My emphasis is on self-actualization. I think astrology can be a tremendous tool in that process, but the process is MOST important. The tool is secondary.'[6] The aim is not that of interpreting the horoscope or forecasting the future. It is employing experiential techniques to activate a reawakening and transformation of the energies represented by the zodiacal signs. 'The aim in the human beings (as in the horoscope) is to integrate these twelve sides of life. We are all learning to recognize all twelve in our lives – not to deny or repress or project any of them.'[7]

The Roots of Astrology

According to conventional history, astrology developed in Mesopotamia from 3000 BC due to the work of some wise men who, after centuries of observation, began to note correlation between events on Earth and movements of planets. The most ancient archaeological materials in all parts of the planet prove however that, no matter how far back we go in human history, astrology has always been there. The astrology of the past did not deal with personalities. It was meant as a study of energy patterns and was expressed collectively. In those times it was not necessary to get involved with complex mathematical calculations to approach the mysteries of the universe. The stars were not only above in the Sky: their energies were accessible here on Earth, and its inhabitants could freely sense them in their bodies, minds and hearts. They were in direct relationship with the planets and stars; they perceived them everywhere and in everything. 'For us, astrology is a mathematical science; for them, it was the intimate knowledge of living energies, as they were aware of the cosmic forces that animate each being. This approach towards planetary forms is the basic key of all ancient thought, of symbolism, religion and mythology.'[8] This basic key has been lost after the disappearance of the traditions of the *Mythic Age*,[9] and with the simultaneous expansion of the ego thought system based on separation.

To try and understand astrology through the belief systems that developed after that Mythic Age, can hardly allow us to know its essential message. Unfortunately no clear documents from those early times seem to be available. That time, far from having actual historical roots on Earth, may easily correspond to the remnants of memory of a dimension which lies beyond our ordinary perception. This makes it pointless to look for it through archaeological research or interpretation of ancient esoteric texts. What is indeed available to everybody is the possibility of connecting with that dimension through an experiential exploration of its domain.

'Astrology is also like the ruins of a great building that once existed. It was a complete science which has been lost. It is neither new nor is it in the process of construction. From the walls that have remained it is not possible to judge how big that building once might have been. Many times truths are realized only to become lost again.'[10] A basic part of the work with astroshamanism is that of retrieving this ancient wisdom in the light of our perception of the present time. In this context it is necessary to employ and integrate all that experiential information which has been cultivated during the times when astrology and shamanism were one.

Astroshamanism

Astrology is undoubtedly the most ancient form of symbolic language, whereas shamanism is the oldest and most widely practised method of healing. In all parts of this planet and in all ages there is evidence of shamanic practices. The word *shaman* comes from *saman,* the Russian transliteration of a term used in Siberia which means somebody 'who sees in the darkness.'[11] A shaman is a human being who, out of his will, is able to enter into an altered state of consciousness to relate with realities which are alien to ordinary human beings and use this connection to get wisdom, ecstasy, power, or for healing purposes. In engaging in their activities shamans move between a so-called *ordinary state of consciousness* and a *non-ordinary,* or *shamanic state of consciousness.* Obscurity, either provided by the night or purposely induced, constitutes the ideal setting for shamanic practices.[12] 'In darkness the distractions of ordinary reality lessen their impingement on consciousness, making it possible for the shaman to focus on the aspects of non-ordinary reality essential to his work. [...] *Shamanic enlightenment* is the literal ability to lighten the darkness, to *see* in that darkness what others cannot perceive.'[13] Yet, differing from mystics or other advanced beings on the spiritual path, shamans do not aim at enlightenment for its own sake. Their main purpose is that of moving into other realms and then coming back to help their community.

In shamanism, as with astrology, there is no separation and everything is perceived as part of the same unity. The chief trait of shamans is their clear perception of that unity. They are very familiar with states of consciousness that allow visions and explorations of the dimensions which exist beyond the physical reality. In order to travel to these spaces, shamans use various tools and receive the support of Spirit Guides (also called guardian spirits, power animals, spirit allies, tutelaries and angels). The relationship with these beings is one of the main characteristics of shamanic culture and represents the basic work of astroshamanism.

Shamanic wisdom includes information on the geography of non-ordinary realities that allows movement in those areas where it is possible to find Spirit Guides, allies, power, grievances, blocks, etc. In astroshamanism, the astrological chart becomes a *Sacred Circle* and takes on its old function as a geographical map of other dimensions. In this context, the chart is not analysed, but it is employed as an aid during the direct exploration of the territories that it portrays.

Astroshamanism does not involve judgements or interpretation through the ordinary functions of the mind; neither does it require the belief in a specific religious doctrine. What matters in this work is laying aside prejudices and fixed ideas so as to open up to an authentic exploration of the mysteries that exist within and without ourselves. Astroshamanism means to access the hidden energy of the zodiacal signs and planets: to feel this energy in the body, the emotions, the mind and spirit. It is not about studying or analysing the theoretical significance of astrological archetypes. It requires that we are available to actually become those archetypes: to experience their power and to move through an intensive process of transformation. This attitude causes a deep inner revolution which it is important to face with gentleness and respect for our rhythms and each part of our being.

In astroshamanism we employ tools which can easily be related to, and integrated in, our contemporary reality. Here the acceptance of traditions of other times and cultures does not imply the evasion from my responsibilities in the current world. Sometimes it can be useful to find inspiration elsewhere and leave the habitual environment in order to discover my true Intent. Once this Intent has been retrieved and reinforced, then

I can decide to make it manifest and accept the need to heal or transform my own original environment. In some way it is easy to play the 'shaman' in nature or feel full of power by emulating the ritual practices of native shamanic cultures. What is difficult is to keep this attitude in ordinary social life and urban environments, and these are the places that need it most. Historically, shamans have always been part of the society where they lived, taking care of its problems, whenever they were allowed to operate. For centuries shamanic cultures have been persecuted in the western world until they were almost entirely exterminated. They have managed to survive in secrecy or through complex esoteric camouflage. Nowadays there seems to be more freedom and this ancient knowledge can re-emerge and be used in our own cultural context and not relegated somewhere else. The world needs shamans able to function on the roads, among the electronic equipment and engines, in the squares and markets of our contemporary society.

1 Hermes Trismegistus (Thrice-Great Hermes) is a mythic figure combining both the features of the Egyptian god Thoth and the Greek Hermes. He is supposed to be the founder of astrology and the tutelary archetype of the western mystery traditions which are based on the integration, interconnectedness and ultimate unity of all aspects of reality. The name Hermes appears to originate from the Greek *herma* or *hermaion*, a monument consisting of an upright stone surrounded by a heap of smaller stones, thus denoting the structure of the Sacred Circle.

2 The term *ego* is Latin for *I* and is used in various contexts with different senses. Here *ego* refers to the entire psyche, or individual self, believed to be a separate identity, distinct from others in its body, emotions, mind and spirit.

3 *A Course in Miracles, Text,* Foundation for Inner Peace, 1992, pp. 586–587.

4 During the years of the great witch hunt and decimation of shamanic cultures in the western world, one of the few possibilities of survival left for shamanic healers was to hide behind the language of astrology or alchemy, as these were widely practised by the physicians of the time and were not regarded as heresies.

5 Carl Gustav Jung, *Collected Works of C.G. Jung: Vol. 13, Alchemical Studies,* Princeton University Press, 1967.

6 Maritha Pottenger, *Encounter Astrology,* TIA, 1978, pp. 7–8.

7 Ibid. p. 17.

8 Alexandre Volguine, *L'esoterismo dell'astrologia*, Xenia, 1996, p. 12.

9 By *Mythic Age* I mean that epoch or 'paradisal age in which human beings' to use the words of Mircea Eliade 'could easily go up to the sky and maintain familiar relations with the gods'. (Mircea Eliade, *Shamanism: Archaic Techniques of Ecstasy*, Princeton University Press, 1972, p. 265).

10 Osho Rajneesh, *Hidden Mysteries,* Rebel Publishing House, 1997, p. 205.

11 In recent decades the term *shaman* has been almost universally adopted by anthropologists and mainstream culture to identify people who were previously referred to with other names, such as *medicine-man, witch, wizard, magician,* etc. In the original language the word *shaman* is pronounced with the stress on the last syllable. The same word may also be related to the Sanskrit word *zramana,* which means somebody who lives a life of religious self-discipline. Another possible connection is with the term *shamah,* which in the ancient Sumerian language means 'that which is highward', and the derivative *shem* describing both a tower or tall conical monument and a shining metal or 'heavenly stone'. 'People of the *shem'* refers to the *Nephilim* – the original Hebrew biblical name (literally meaning 'those who had descended' and unproperly translated as 'giants' in the common English translation) of those beings, or *demigods* who, according to certain authors were the result of the interbreeding between the *gods,* or *extraterrestrials,* which the Bible calls Elohim, and the daughters of men.

12 Darkness enhances the production of *melatonin,* the hormonal secretion (often called 'hormone of darkness') of the pineal gland. This gland, shaped like a pine-cone and with the size of a grain of puffed rice, is at the base of the brain. Biologists regard it as an evolutionary relic of an eye, which still operates in many lizards. The pineal gland is traditionally associated with our highest spiritual function, with the 'third eye' (*ajna* chakra), organ of inner vision and clairvoyance, or the crown (*sahasrara* chakra). Darkness increases its activity and, as a result, intuitive knowledge and shamanic states of consciousness.

13 Michael Harner, *The Way of the Shaman*, Harper, 1990, p. 22.

CHAPTER 2

THE SACRED CIRCLE

The zodiacal circle employed in astroshamanism is a *Sacred Circle*. The chief feature of the Sacred Circle is that it allows the establishment of a direct connection with the *Spirit Guide* (the Inner Guide, the Centre, the Divine or whatever name you give to That) instead of a relationship of mediation through a *guru* or spiritual authority. There are many ways of working with the Sacred Circle. They are the result of the labour of wise men and women who, throughout the ages, have contributed to bringing spiritual awareness and healing on this planet. Each method has its own tools and connects with a specific culture or lineage. The material that is available on the original use of the Sacred Circle is however very rare. This is due to the ancient refusal to transmit such spiritual teachings in written form. What is mostly known at the moment is usually the result of research or visions from present day scholars or shamans.

Mattie Davis-Wolfe and David Thomson describe the Sacred Circle, or *Medicine Wheel* (as it is often called according to some Native American traditions), as follows:

> *The wheel is anchored in the four cardinal directions, which arise from the Earth's ongoing relationship with the Sun and Moon. This revolving around each other of the Earth, Sun and Moon, spiralling through space, sets up the energy pattern for all other relationships on Earth. This is the source of Earth's abiding regularities and boundless diversity. The Wheel of the Year, therefore, can teach us*

> *about our deepest natures, as beings of the Earth in continual relationship with all other life and forms. But the Wheel is not merely a tool, it is a pattern for a sacred way of life – a way of beauty and balance. The myths, rituals and celebrations of early people were in alignment with the patterns that were appropriate to the time of day or season of the year. The intent of these occasions was more to bring people in tune with the energies than just to celebrate together. The repetitive nature and larger pattern of participation reminded the people that they were part of an organic dynamic rhythm. The health of the larger whole was directly dependent upon the dedication of each element to its own nature and the quality of its participation in the great plan of the circle of life. Participation in the larger whole was a dynamic interactive process. After we opened to the energies of the circle, we could go deeper into its lessons. For instance, it is possible to enter into the energies of the circle, and just go round and round in the same track without ever changing or learning. But opening to the deeper lesson teaches us about the spiral – the circle that opens so that each journey around is different than the one before, just as each first morning of Winter is never the same as the years before. We learn that we do return to the same places, but as different people because of the experiences had and lessons learned along the way.*[1]

The Ordinary Reality

The major grievances of the world are the result of how I perceive the world and not of what is indeed happening there. The cause of any problem that I seem to experience comes from a state of hallucination. The producers of such a state, who, in an ancient time long forgotten, I myself created, are based in a subtle and hidden dimension. The ordinary reality, as I perceive it, is but a huge and intricate virtual screen which operates on multiple levels. Its origins and developments extend far beyond the understanding and scope of the established functioning of the mind. Trapped in the pen of the binary system and of identification with their physical bodies, human beings eat up a fodder of sin, guilt and fear, as they watch the soap opera of life being repeated over and over. Yet such a mirage is so insane and unreal that attentive eyes cannot help discovering gaps all over the place. Although the operators at the projector do their best to patch it up, the absurd illusion of this misperception may reveal itself at any moment. It is like a boasting block of ice showing off its solidity as long as the temperature is below zero and yet inevitably starting to thaw and melt away in warmer weather. To be aware of the hallucination, to release it and disclose the truth which lies beyond is the basic purpose of astroshamanism. This aim is acted out within the ego framework of the mind through the employment of a specific strategic structure composed of *Twelve Sectors,* i.e. twelve essential energy patterns that, together with the Four Directions, form the *horizontal axis* of the Sacred Circle. The *vertical axis* is represented by the *above* (Higher World), the *below* (Lower World) and the *centre* (Middle World). This structure constitutes the projector of the virtual reality which thrives in this universe of multiple dimensions. It is the operating team directing the comedy of life which a part of the mind produces in its attempt to deceive itself. I cannot complain about such a team for, although it is easy to forget and play the victim, I contributed to creating and placing it there. Well, at times it looks like an intricate and overwhelming mess. Yet, there is an insane logic in it to which, somewhere, I do possess the keys. My function is to undo this mess as I have realised that the more I go into it, the more I find further mess. I was mistaken and I made a fallacious choice. Yet I can choose again.

The Structure of the Sacred Circle

Each sector of the Sacred Circle describes a specific group of energies, or major archetypes. The examination of the astrological chart can give more clues about the ways and times in which these energies express themselves. Yet this, although useful, does not constitute a priority. A sector designates a major living organic unity with whom it is possible to establish a direct relationship without having to meet astrological technical requirements or having specific intellectual skills. If there are problems with a particular sector, or if I feel anger or discomfort in its presence, this is usually a kind of energy that I have repressed, dissociated or expelled from my awareness. In order to find my totality, sooner or later I need to retrieve it. The original aim of the structure of the Twelve Sectors is to support the healing from the plague of separation. This involves the acceptance, recognition and integration of each part of myself as it is represented by each sector. This requires more from me than

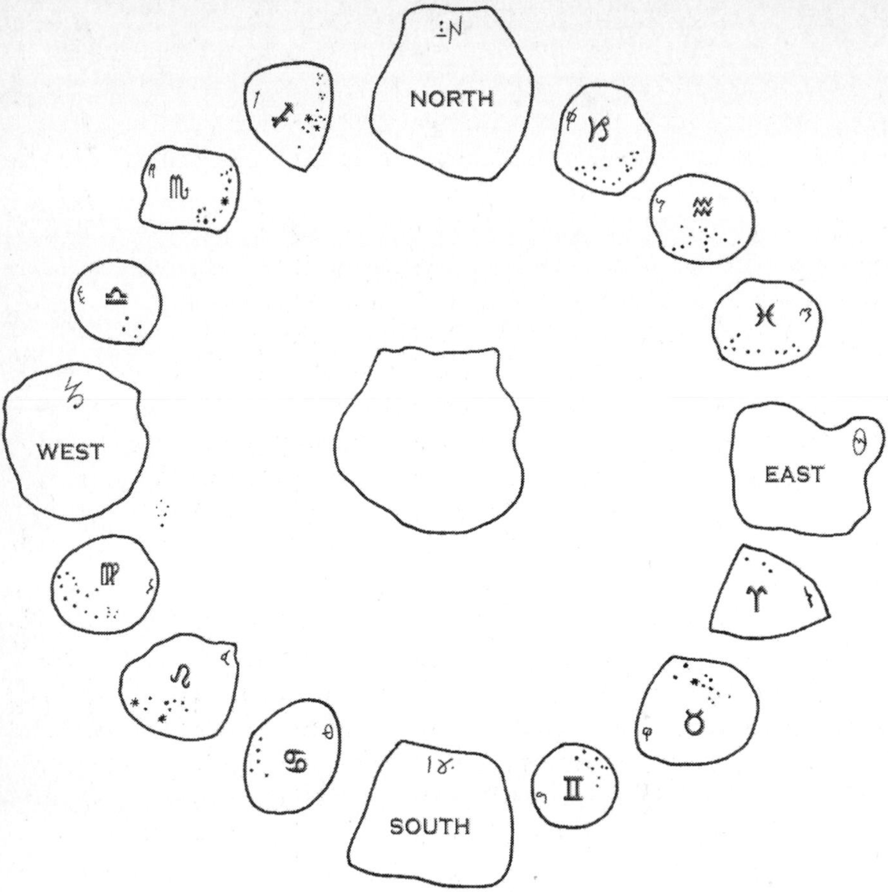

Figure 1: The Astroshamanic Sacred Circle

E: East	S: South	W: West	N: North
1 Aries ♈ Sector 1 Mars ♂	4 Cancer ♋ Sector 4 Moon ☽	7 Libra ♎ Sector 7 Venus ♀	10 Capricorn ♑ Sector 10 Saturn ♄
2 Taurus ♉ Sector 2 Venus ♀	5 Leo ♌ Sector 5 Sun ☉	8 Scorpio ♏ Sector 8 Mars ♂ Pluto ♇	11 Aquarius ♒ Sector 11 Saturn ♄ Uranus ♅
3 Gemini ♊ Sector 3 Mercury ☿	6 Virgo ♍ Sector 6 Mercury ☿ Asteroids	9 Sagittarius ♐ Sector 9 Jupiter ♃	12 Pisces ♓ Sector 12 Jupiter ♃ Neptune ♆

merely acknowledging or learning a philosophical and spiritual truth, that of the unity of existence (although this can certainly help). Until I have had a direct experience of my nature, with its deepest fears and desires, and of what exists beyond ordinary reality, with all the layers of lies and stupidities which clog my human perception, I cannot reach the realisation of this truth.

The ability to be a spiritual seeker consists in being able to journey through the various sectors, moving from one world to the other and keeping the connection with the vertical axis. Once, in epic times, according to the myths of many traditions, this type of experience was widely available. Then something happened that created a separation and the consequent severance of the dialogue between human beings, the Three Worlds and the Twelve Sectors. 'After the interruption of the *easy communications* that, at the dawn of time, existed between mankind and the gods, certain privileged beings (and first of all the shamans),' writes Mircea Eliade, 'preserved the power to actualize, for their own persons, the connection with the upper regions.'[2] A lot can be argued about the objective reality of these spaces and their content: whether they are projections from the unconscious or extensions of the higher self. According to Michael Harner, the shaman does not consider non-ordinary realities as a projection of his mind, rather, it is the mind itself which 'is being used to pass through a door into another reality, which exists independently of that mind.'[3] Shamanic wisdom is based on the understanding of the mysteries related to inter-dimensional passages, and on the experience that in the universe there is something that goes beyond the material and intellectual sphere. 'Only they [the shamans] know how to make an ascent through the "central opening"; only they transform a cosmo-theological concept into a *concrete mystical experience*'.[4] What counts here is not the blind acceptance of a specific vision of the universe, but its experiential employment and direct investigation. For the shaman, after all, the objective of the journey is not the journey in itself, but the application of the power and wisdom which is acquired in that context to bring healing and harmony to the ordinary reality.

The existence of non-ordinary realities has always been considered and experienced in all human history. Black Elk, a *Lakota* medicine-man, describes them as follows 'the true world which lies behind this, so that each thing that we see is like a shadow of that world.'[5] According to shamanism, these realities are authentic dimensions of space and time or of something which is beyond space and time. They are inhabited by beings who are as *real* (and often more *real* or less illusive!) than the men, women, animals and plants who live on Earth. During the history of humankind, many individuals have had experiences with such dimensions. The descriptions they gave have frequently been manipulated or obscured by their tradition or culture of origin, and have reached us through different kinds of expressions. These diverse ways of describing the experience of reality are defined in astroshamanism as the Three Levels.

The Three Levels

Astroshamanism strategically considers three basic levels of which I am giving here a brief, rudimentary outline. The experiential understanding of the levels is a key in astroshamanic work. According to this vision, each human being relates to all three levels with different degrees of awareness. In considering the levels, please be aware that each one of them consists of further sublevels (which tend to repeat the patterns of the three main levels).

Level 1 is related to the physical realm and the identification with bodies or three-dimensional forms. It constitutes the end product of the illusive reality created by the ego and the ultimate manifestation of the thought of separation projected by Level 2. According to the nature of its sublevels it employs different expressions. The current ordinary human perspective is basically geocentric and refers to the Earth, its tribal consciousness and dominant traditions (religious, cultural, social, political, etc.). It includes all the earth-centred conditioning inherited from the ancestors of this planet and in particular that which is prevalent in the specific time-space environment of the ego involved. It generally excludes or disregards whatever is beyond the physical plan of the Earth, any understanding contrary to its ongoing conditioning or awareness of life on other dimensions, realms, planets or galaxies (at least for the time being). It represents the *personality* level and the conventional reality as it is experienced by most humans and also the way in which some specific dominant ego thought forms, or *non-human* beings, want it to be experienced (although this latter belief is inconceivable at the current Level 1 of most of humankind). Its purpose is to protect and perpetuate the experience of this reality. This level corresponds to the process of *First Attention* – i.e. the attention focused on the physical plane and identified with the part which acts in daily life (the one which is called *I*) – and can be astrologically associated with the zodiacal signs or the traditional rulerships of the planets. Advanced expressions of Level 1 have heliocentric, galactic, universal or multi-dimensional perspectives and relate to the solar system, the galaxy, the universe and the non-ordinary realities of which the Earth is just a minor, fragmented part.

Level 2 is associated with the mental realm and with the split mind which dominates or affects most seen and unseen beings currently living in this universe. It includes the ego thought system based on the illusion of separation and the residual memories or reflections of thought systems founded on unity. Level 2 constitutes the causative source of Level 1 and the agent of choice between either the preservation and expansion or retrieval and undoing of the fragmented universe produced by the ego. It encompasses all thought forms inherited and distributed over the physical universe and all possible dimensions. It generally tends to exclude, discourage or be in conflict with, whatever is not related to the process of expansion and preservation of the illusion of separation. It is also inclined to operate for the release of this illusion especially when this entails a state of antagonism with the illusion itself. Level 2 represents the *soul* level and the reality as it is experienced by *superior* beings in the universe and by a small minority of human beings on Earth. This level corresponds to the process of *Secondary Attention* – i.e. the part focused on what is normally neglected or considered irrational, subjective, based on inner plane realities (often a source of disturbance, relationship issues, health problems, addictions, distractions, etc.) – and may be astrologically associated with the houses or the unorthodox rulerships of the planets according to esoteric astrology. Astroshamanically it coincides with the *Epic of the Sacred Cone*. It is caught between Levels 1 and 3, and constitutes both the ego's secret thriving base for separation and the itinerary which paves the way to the golden path to the original awareness of unity.

Level 3 is related to the spiritual realm and represents the access to the dimension beyond the illusion of separation and the ego system as it is represented by Levels 1 and 2. Its reality is based on unity, love, peace, joy and other terms which are far beyond any attempt of description in human languages. It is the pure echo of our original nature as truly divine beings, Sons of God, Spirit Tribe, Light of the World. It ranges from the *higher mental* level to the *buddhic, spiritual* and *monadic* levels, representing the final programme, or itinerary, of the journey back to the full awareness of unity. It inspires and totally stands by the final process of undoing or releasing the universe based on separation and is the gate to what lies beyond the illusion of this universe. This level corresponds to the *Tertiary Attention* – i.e. the awareness of the interconnection of all life and the experience of unity (the centre of the cyclone, or a part able to witness both primary and secondary attention) – and may be astrologically associated with the planets or the unorthodox rulerships of the Hierarchical Order according to esoteric astrology.

To sum all this up again and phrase it differently, Level 1 considers its area of reference virtually as the only possible location. This means that what is not part of that area, either does not exist, is denied, repressed, ridiculed, fought or diplomatically handled to keep it away. Each planet has its own Level 1, as well as each country, tradition, sex, religion, large group or individual. Level 1 is a provisional symbolic device aimed at serving either an Intent connected with the Function (see Chapter 3) or an *intent* that separates from the Function and generates confusion between symbols and reality. Once Level 1 has served its Intent, it needs to be released, undone or forgiven (which are all synonyms) in order to give space to Level 2. Level 2 is associated with the individual's specific vision or, in other terms, to that which connects with a tradition not acknowledged by Level 1 and which exists at a larger or deeper or higher degree of awareness. Also Level 2 is meant to be released in the end so as to allow Level 3 to take over. This last level is the ultimate symbol and represents the gate to reality. Such a process, here roughly described in a linear way, has rather a circular and spiral motion. It is like a lift moving up and down, every time carrying new people or material and advancing in its reawakening process. The distinctive feature of shamans is that they are capable of shifting to all three levels at will and often perceive them simultaneously.

The Vertical Axis and the Three Worlds

The chief trait of astroshamanism is the experience of shamanic states of consciousness and the direct relationship with Spirit Guides and all possible ordinary or non-ordinary realities of which the sectors of the Sacred Circle represent the reference space. The modalities of the relationship with these realities have reached us in a very fragmented way through the shamanic culture which survived at the periphery of the globe, the secret work of mystery schools, the teachings of some enlightened masters and, most of all, through the connection with other dimensions and states of perception, which is always available to those individuals who are willing to have this experience. The astroshamanic cosmology employs the classical esoteric and shamanic division to *vertical* and *horizontal axes*. The vertical axis is traditionally composed of the Three Worlds: *the Higher World, the Lower World, the Middle World.*[6]

The Higher World, also called *Upper World, Sky, Heaven, Nation of the Great Star, Spiritual Realm,* is made up of different layers traditionally inhabited by spiritual masters, gods, planets, stars, cosmic beings from other planets, solar systems or galaxies. The journey to this area offers the opportunity to rediscover our most ancient past and to receive information on the actual reasons for our presence on Earth. For some shamanic traditions the physical universe is a projection, or forgery, of the Higher World. This means that the latter is not in the universe of stars or galaxies that are observable through telescopes, but in another dimension. In the Higher World it is easy to experience a sense of lightness and strong connection with the whole, and to receive visions, guidance or suggestions for the fulfilment of one's mission on Earth.

The Lower World, or *Underworld,* is traditionally the realm of instinctive understanding where animal, vegetal and mineral powers abide together with all the beings related with the deepest mysteries of this planet and other similar dimensions. Here it is possible to receive help and guidance on the reality which is acknowledged by most beings on Earth. A shamanic journey in the Lower World is often undertaken to connect with animal spirits or ancestral guides. According to the type of level at work, this world is also the traditional place where some beings go when they leave their physical body or where bodies proceed when the beings that inhabit them depart.

The Middle World corresponds to the so-called ordinary reality, as it is perceived by most human beings. It also coincides with a non-ordinary transposition of that reality, where it is possible to travel back and forth into the history of humankind and the planet. The exploration of this world allows movement through the geographical areas of the globe to locate plants, stones, power tools and points, etc. The Middle World often contains trapped beings, rotten thought forms and various grievances which need to be released to allow the communication between the other two worlds.

According to the *Epic of the Sacred Cone,* the Middle World represents the circular base of two spiral cones placed one on top of the other (see Figure 2). The upper cone is associated with the Higher World, whereas the lower cone corresponds to the Lower World. The cosmology of the Three Worlds strategically depicts the multi-dimensional reality where our planet, solar system, galaxy and all the known or unknown universe are located. This reality is defined as the *Grey Sphere,* or *Sphere of Light and Darkness,* and constitutes one of the three multi-dimensional spheres of the cosmology of the Sacred Cone. The Grey Sphere and its three worlds represent the area of connection between two additional spheres: *White Sphere,* or *Sphere of Light,* and *Black Sphere,* or *Sphere of Darkness.* The epic function of the Grey Sphere consists of facilitating the connection between spheres and in gradually undoing itself so as to allow the ultimate merging of the White and Black Spheres. The Grey Sphere embodies specific areas aimed at supporting this function. In this context the Epic identifies three main strategic locations: *Handor* for the White Sphere,

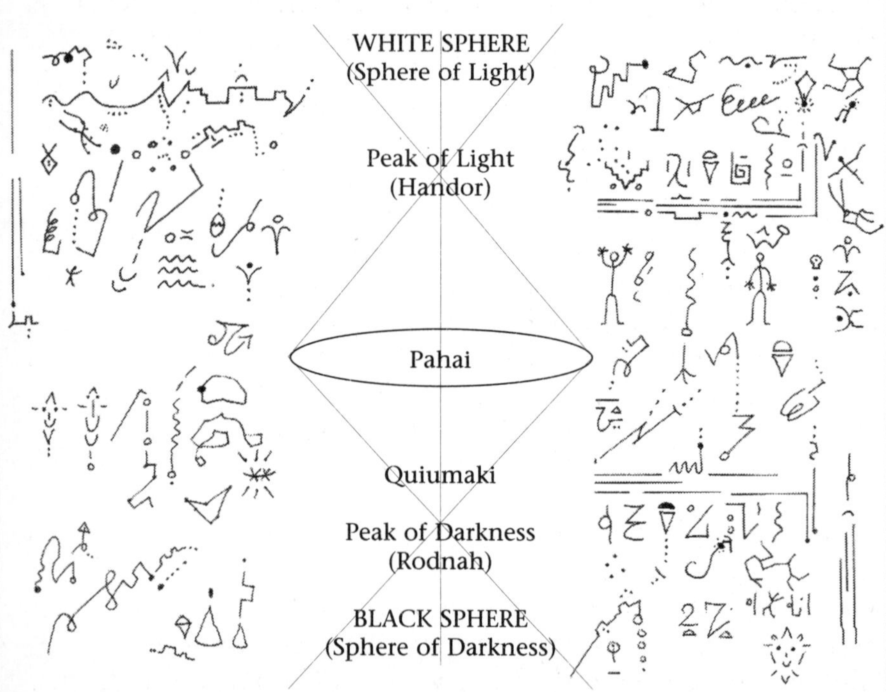

Figure 2: The Cosmology of the Sacred Cone

Rodnah for the Black Sphere and *Pahai* for the Grey Sphere. The first two areas represent the *Peak,* or access gate, to the sphere to which they refer and the apex of the two cones of the Grey Sphere. The third area (Pahai) is the system of connection between such cones and paves the way to the vertical axis.

In astrological terms and broadly speaking, the Middle World can be astrologically related to the seven traditional planets (Sun, Moon, Mercury, Venus, Mars, Jupiter, Saturn), the Higher World to Uranus and Neptune, and the Lower World to Pluto. This is not however an absolute identification for each planet reproduces in itself the division of the three Worlds. The vertical cosmology of the Sacred Circle is represented by the Three Worlds and by their connection through a central axis. This axis is located at the Centre of the Circle and is known with a large variety of names such as *vertical axis, Tree of the World, Great Tree, Cosmic Mountain, Axis Mundi, cross, mount Meru, mount Sinai, Yggdrasil, pyramid.*

All major mystical, shamanic and esoteric traditions on this planet have employed cartographies mapping the vertical axis and the different stages encountered during its exploration. In the Indian system, for example, the vertical axis is seen as the representation of the spinal route along which flows the energy referred to as *kundalini*. This energy is described as a female snake that lies coiled and sleeping at the base of the spine. In the majority of human beings it remains dormant for most of the time, whereas in those who manage to wake it up or unconsciously have it awakened, it rises up and attempts to pierce the six centres, or *chakras,* located along the spine. If the channel is clear and there are no blocks the energy ascends until it reaches the seventh centre and gives access to that experience known as *enlightenment*. This accomplishment is regarded as the ultimate freedom, or the reawakening to unity from the illusion of separation. If there are blocks along the spinal route, the energy creates a pressure that can be experienced as pain or erratic conditions on a physical, emotional, mental or spiritual level.

Astroshamanically the structure of the vertical axis reflects in the human body through the exchange between the centre of the *head* (Higher World) and that of the *belly* (Lower World). These areas are related to forces that are beyond the perception of ordinary human beings. The key of connection between these areas is represented by the *heart* (Middle World) which operates as a bridge between Higher and Lower Worlds. In this context bodies may appear as *space-time suits* or symbolic representations of a symbol of a further symbol and so on, until *something* which is not a symbol is reached. This can be symbolically described as *love, light, unity, ecstasy, God*. Sometimes this long symbolic itinerary does not take much to unravel. Occasionally it follows a long chain of symbolic sequences which need much time to be unveiled. Your own experience with shamanic journeys will

Provisional Reference Chart of the Four Directions

Direction	Element & Realm	Animals	Minerals	Plants	Colour	Season	Totem Spirit	Part of day
East	Fire, spiritual	wolf, eagle, predatory animals	iron	tobacco	red	Spring	*Ruha*	dawn
South	Earth, physical	dormouse, deer, peaceful animals	serpentine, jasper	sage, patchouli	green	Summer	*Ratah*	noon
West	Water, emotional	snake, reptiles, fish, sea animals	obsidian, river stone	cedar, sandalwood, camphor	blue	Autumn	*Rogah*	sunset
North	Air, mental	seagull, birds	crystal	lavender, sweetgrass	yellow	Winter	*Riallah*	midnight

Provisional Reference Chart of the Twelve Sectors

Sector	Sign	Planets	Element	Animals	Minerals	Totem Spirit	Colour
1	Aries ♈	Mars	Fire	hawk, badger	red jasper	Kahe Pah	red
2	Taurus ♉	Venus	Earth	beaver, bull	green jasper	Rata Sahe Pah	red-orange
3	Gemini ♊	Mercury	Air	deer, monkey, jay	tiger's eye	Mahe Rahe Tahe	orange
4	Cancer ♋	Moon	Water	crab, rabbit	carnelian	Quiushade	orange-yellow
5	Leo ♌	Sun	Fire	lion, peacock	citrine, amber	Surahim Tahe	yellow
6	Virgo ♍	Mercury	Earth	squirrel, bear	adventurine	Kahesepoh Sadeh	yellow-green
7	Libra ♌	Venus	Air	raven, owl	rose quartz	Ataherah	green
8	Scorpio ♏	Mars, Pluto	Water	scorpion, snake	malachite, hematite	Harassadoah	green-blue
9	Sagittarius ♐	Jupiter	Fire	elk, horse, dolphin	sapphire	Nivaya Sadhu	blue
10	Capricorn ♑	Saturn	Earth	snow goose, goat	onyx, green tourmaline	Sauter Kitaya	blue-violet
11	Aquarius ♒	Saturn, Uranus	Air	otter, seagull	silver, azurite	Uriah Tapeh	violet
12	Pisces ♓	Jupiter, Neptune	Water	whale, mountain lion	flourite, turquoise	Taepeh	violet-red

provide true understanding of this. There is no point at this stage in wasting time trying to grasp with the ordinary mind what is far beyond its reach. Any attempt to explain such matters is bound to crush what it is trying to explain. Be also aware that all the preceding information can be very easily contaminated by *false guides* (see Chapter 6, False Guides), creating diversions from your journey. A major tool and learning device which can be of help in the comprehension of the vertical axis is your physical body. Connect with that and pay attention to the subtle information that it carries. Your body can function as an astroshamanic map. Listen to it and tune in to its right frequency. Also be aware that what occurs at the physical level tends to be the direct result of what happens in the mental realm. It is this latter level that ultimately requires your maximum attention.

As regards the preceding charts, please be aware that there are many divergent views in the allocation of animals, minerals, seasons, colours or elements to Directions and Sectors. These can change according to each tradition, native people and even individual. The correspondences given in this text do not purport in any way to be more powerful or better than others and are merely provided as examples.

The Horizontal Axis and the Twelve Sectors

Next to the vertical axis, represented by the Three Worlds, spreads the horizontal axis which is pictured as a circle with four major directions and twelve sectors. Each direction has its basic archetypal nature which relates to a season of the year, an element, three sectors – zodiacal signs – and various animals, plants, minerals, colours and beings. There are different types of Sacred Circle and each of them has its specific traits. The correspondences employed to identify the Four Directions change according to various traditions. As far as I am concerned no model can be considered as right or wrong. Usually correspondences vary according to the nature of the geographical locations where they develop. For example, in the areas where the sea is found on the western side, West may become the direction for the element of Water. In astroshamanism different models can be used. The one that I employ belongs to one of the main traditions of reference in the *Epic* and it is also common to many other systems. Although there are reasons to support it, for the purpose of astroshamanic work I will consider this model as simply strategic.

If you divide each of the Four Directions by three, you get the Twelve Sectors. Each one of the sectors corresponds to a specific time of the year and may refer to one of the twelve supposed helices of the original DNA.[7] The Twelve Sectors are popularly known as the *Zodiac*. This word comes from the Greek *zo* (i.e. 'animal' as in the English word *zoo*) and probably means 'the circle of the animals'. The Zodiac is one of the most widespread symbols, and examples of its arrangement can be found in all ages and cultures. In ancient numerology, the number twelve represented the structure of space-time division, i.e. the product of the Four Directions and the Three Worlds. In all traditions there are abundant traces of this system. In the Bible the holy Jerusalem is described as having 'twelve gates, and at the gates twelve angels, and names written thereon, which are *the names* of the twelve tribes of the children of Israel; on the east three gates; on the north three gates; on the south three gates; and on the west three gates. And the wall of the city had twelve foundations, and in them the names of the twelve apostles of the Lamb.' (Revelation 21:12–14). In most shamanic cultures there are twelve rites of passage, or stages of initiation, and twelve are the basic gods, goddesses and heroes of most religious traditions. According to Erodotus, the year was divided by twelve by the Egyptians who defined the structure of the twelve divinities which was later employed in the Greek and Roman pantheon.[8]

The characteristics of each sector are astrologically represented by the symbols of the zodiacal signs, whereas in many shamanic traditions *totems* are employed. A totem is an energetic unit that allows direct communication with spiritual and non-physical beings through the employment of a physical form (plant, animal, mineral, etc.). In the Algonquin languages *totem* corresponds to *otem,* 'sign' or 'family, tribe', preceded by the personal pronoun *t.* This word is now widely applied in anthropology to identify the primal ancestor or hereditary seal of a tribe or tradition. Totems are energetic sensors that through a physical form (plant, animal, mineral, object, planet, star, image of a god) facilitate the understanding of non-physical forms and pure archetypal forces. In astroshamanism we refer to twelve basic Totem Spirits constituting the twelve essential archetypes and shape-shifting into numerous forms.

One of the major technical differences between the zodiacal circle and most traditional Sacred Circles is that in the former, sectors proceed anti-clockwise, whereas in the latter they move clockwise. Sacred Circles are in alignment with the patterns of seasonal cycles and the time of day on Earth, while the Zodiac, since it represents the imaginary band that surrounds our planet, is more connected with the Sky and the measuring of the apparent motion of celestial bodies as they are seen from Earth. This difference of perspective puts in evidence a major strategic difference between the spiritual vision of ancient people and that of the religions which have prevailed in recent times. The Earth-centred cultures support the descent of Spirit on Earth and the observation of the Sacred Circle from above to below. In traditional medicine wheels the circle is *put down to earth* so as to allow the energy of celestial bodies to be grounded on this planet. As a matter of fact, this energy, once it reaches the Earth and is transformed by this impact, ascends to the Sky, then descends and so on through a constant and unbiased exchange between the Higher and the Lower Worlds. The prevailing approach of modern civilisation seems to emphasize the process of ascent toward Spirit and the observation from below to above. This perspective, like the previous one, can easily cause imbalance when awareness of the opposite process is lacking. A common trend for many recent spiritual traditions has been that of overstressing the ascent to the Sky as a way of *running away* from Earth. The *Epic of the Sacred Cone*, as well as most shamanic traditions, teaches that, before moving anywhere else, we need to encompass this planet and become one with it. As Ur Kraab says: 'We can return to Father Sky only if we take Mother Earth with us.'[9]

The Astroshamanic System of the Twelve Sectors

The advantage of the model of the Twelve Sectors is that, besides being very old and widespread, it represents the easiest symbolic structure for most human beings. Almost everybody has some familiarity with the twelve zodiacal signs, considers a year of twelve months or regularly looks at a watch with a circle of twelve numbers. In astroshamanism the Twelve Sectors represent the various ways and energies which lead to the Centre of the Sacred Circle. In this Centre there is no sense of separation as everything is perceived as part of the same whole. Sectors are emanations of the Centre aimed at making this Centre understandable to minds conditioned by the illusion of separation. One way to explain this is that, as there is a state of hallucination at work (where I perceive the sectors as separated), I can access the Centre only through a system which is acknowledged by this hallucination. With respect to this, the

Centre has created a *Plan* that, starting from my distorted perception and with the guidance of those (Spirit Guides) who are not affected by this hallucination, enables me to return to my true perception (the unity of the whole). In this book I call this Plan, the *Plan of Salvation* or the *Game Resolution*.

The Sacred Circle is the container of all possible situations in human and non-human experiences. The most comprehensive spectrum of existence is described in this system. This means that, no matter how far from the Centre I am, my exact location can be spotted in the Circle and from there I can find my way to the Centre. From this perspective in each sector there is a passage that enables me to reach the Centre and this means that I have always the possibility of accessing the Centre, no matter where I am.

In brief, astroshamanic work consists of acknowledging my highest Intent and the Centre from where it emanates, so as to move in each sector to find the access to that Centre. It is a systematic and cyclic operation that can be practised either with or without awareness. Every living creature takes part in this process. Some choose to consciously commit and actively work for it or to surrender to the flow of its events, while others pretend not to be involved and assume the role of victims. All trails inevitably lead to the same Centre and are equally respected and honoured as such. Lessons are repeated until they are fully understood. From this perspective there is no pressure and I have ample choice to elect the time that I take for my journey, though in certain circumstances my true nature can employ any means to confront me with such a choice. For example, sometimes unpredictable and dramatic events occur to release situations of block, stagnation or fear with which the person involved is unable or unwilling to cope. Although these episodes may appear as painful or unfortunate, they are crucial for opening gates in the consciousness and boosting the spiritual journey of certain people. Of course, it is also possible to choose much gentler lessons and to work in co-operation with Spirit Guides and Totem Spirits. 'Everyone is responsible for his own existence, and nobody has the right to attribute to others this responsibility, the original astrology has this concept well rooted in itself, and every astrological analysis leads only to one basic conclusion: that you, and only you, are the ruler of your destiny, of yourself and of the whole universe. All you can do is to pretend that this is not true.'[10]

There are numerous ways to work with the Sacred Circle and each one deserves respect and honour. The fact that it is sometimes better to stick to one model does not at all imply that others are wrong. A model is a strategic structure and, as such, no model can purport to be the only true system. The one that I will briefly describe in the next chapter is appropriate not because it is the *right* model, but because it may allow the establishment of a common structure upon which the work can develop. Later on, through your direct experience and practice, you may further elaborate this method or, if you receive specific guidance and insight, move to a different one.

1 Mattie Davis-Wolfe; David Thomson, 'Introduction', pp. 2–3, in *Walking the Sacred Wheel,* Sacred Circles Institute, 1995.

2 Mircea Eliade, *Shamanism: Archaic Techniques of Ecstasy,* Princeton University Press, 1972, p. 265.

3 'The Ancient Wisdom in Shamanic Cultures', an interview with Michael Herner conducted by Gary Doore, in Shirley Nicholson (ed), *Shamanism: an Expanded View of Reality,* Theosophical Publishing House, 1987, p. 2.

4 Eliade, *Shamanism,* p. 265.

5 John C. Neihardt, *Black Elk Speaks: Being the Life Story of a Holy Man of the Oglala Sioux,* University of Nebraska Press, 1961.

6 Please be aware that although these worlds have names related to specific vertical positions, this is merely to adjust to our limited sense of direction and does not imply that their actual location corresponds to the way they are described.

7 According to a specific reading of the *Epic of the Sacred Cone*, the current ordinary human DNA is limited to two helices, or sectors, due to the block caused by the *Paheka Rubhe*. This term, which can be translated as the 'Binary Net of Totem Spirits', indicates the 144 combinations of the 12 *Paheka* (as they are *epically* called) or Totem Spirits' double polarities that prevent the expansion of human perception. Undoing these combinations and re-establishing the twelve-helix system is one of the major strategic tasks of advanced astroshamanic work.

8 Herodotus, *The Histories*, II, 4.

9 As a matter of fact this could also be read as 'We can return to Mother Sky only if we take Father Earth with us'.

10 Haram, *Manuale laico di astrologia,* Savelli, 1979, p. 21.

CHAPTER 3

INTENT AND FUNCTION*

The word *Intent* is often employed in this text. It indicates the purest expression of my purpose in life, or in a specific situation in space or time, as it is understandable within the separate reality of the ego. The definition of the Intent creates a field of energy that allows me to take total responsibility and to attract the forces that are needed. 'The value of deciding in advance what you want to happen is simply that you will perceive the situation as a means to *make* it happen. You will therefore make every effort to overlook what interferes with the accomplishment of your objective, and concentrate on everything that helps you meet it.' *(ACIM, Text, p. 366)* The Intent is a basic tool for inner transformation when it aligns with the Function, that is when I cease to use my will to nourish the ego and employ it to contribute to the realisation of my true purpose in life. The word *Function,* also often employed here, identifies itself with *forgiveness,* meant as release, undoing or

* The thought system which mainly inspires this chapter and also further passages of this work is that of *A Course in Miracles®* (often abbreviated here as *ACIM*). The primary focus of *ACIM* is that of undoing the perception of separation, and this is also the purpose of astroshamanism and of other spiritual disciplines. Please be aware that this does not imply that astroshamanism is based on, or associated, with *ACIM*. Ideas from *ACIM* are given mainly because they have deeply inspired me in the past and constitute part of my own spiritual background. All the references to *ACIM* that appear in this text come from my understanding and are not necessarily endorsed by the copyright holders of *ACIM*.

healing of the illusion of separation. Forgiveness is the highest aim for human beings and represents, in the words of *A Course in Miracles*, the key to happiness. As such, it is a Function based on my choice and does not depend on God. 'God does not forgive because He has never condemned. And there must be condemnation before forgiveness is necessary. Forgiveness is the great need of this world, but that is because it is a world of illusions. Those who forgive are thus releasing themselves from illusions, while those who withhold forgiveness are binding themselves to them. As you condemn only yourself, so do you forgive only yourself.' *(ACIM, Workbook, p.73)*

The Intent is a basic requirement for inner journeys and spiritual practices as it allows clarification of the true motivation behind any shamanic enterprise. The fact that the Intent needs to be connected with the Function does not mean that their content is the same. In astroshamanism, the Intent is simply what, according to my present awareness, I honestly want. It does not matter what it is, or whether it seems egocentric or silly. What counts is to establish what I want and what I am ready to give in exchange. 'The goal must be formulated clearly and kept in mind.' *(ACIM, Text, p. 66)* When I am clear and truthful regarding my Intent, and commit to realising it, results will not wait for long. Any shamanic work is based on this premise. The ego never truly commits because it is not ultimately convinced about what it wants. The ego only knows what it does not want: this is the only thing on which it is very clear. And this is the reason why most human beings, thinking of what they do not want, lose their purpose in life and support what they fear.

The adherence to the Intent allows me to face my operativity, to set the energies in motion and to accept making mistakes so as to correct them as my perception gradually expands. Thought is creative and gives form to my reality. Successful people are aware of the power of the mind and know how to use it. This does not mean that their path is necessarily spiritual. Sometimes, if I work well, I can receive some rewards from the ego. However, if they are not connected with my Function, such 'gifts' soon fade away as clouds. It is difficult to assess general values as regards the content of the Intent. What makes the Intent sacred is not its content, but its availability to connect with the Function. It is like the following prayer: 'Oh Spirit, my perception is limited and I am aware that I do not fully know what I want. From what I can perceive of the luminous part in me, I feel that I want… and I am ready to work so as to manifest that. This is my Intent, that I connect with the Function to signify, that at any moment, I am ready to surrender to the highest will.'

The Ego System

I am the only one who can choose whether to employ the world in order to remain in a state of fear, where I am the victim of circumstances, or to consider it as a learning path to retrieve my memory and reach out for my truth. To support the latter choice, we employ apparently different devices which ultimately identify only one remedy: the Function of forgiveness. Through the practice of forgiveness, I let go of the past and, with it, all prejudices, fears and grievances that the ego has placed between me and God. God is here meant as the love within myself, my true source where I acknowledge myself as part of the whole. The ego is my separate identity, based on fear and on an illusive perception of what I am. In order to understand what the significance of forgiveness is, I am going to explore here the structure of the ego as it is described by *A Course in Miracles*.[1]

The ego system runs around three key concepts: *sin* (or *separation*), *guilt* and *fear*. *Sin* is defined as *lack of love. (ACIM, Text, p. 11)* As, according to *A Course in Miracles*, only love is real; sin is not a negative action that requires punishment, but an error or hallucination to correct. Sin is, briefly, the belief of being separate from God and all that exists.

The inevitable consequence of sin is *guilt*: a sense of inner unworthiness due to something wrong I did or something right I did not do. Guilt is not only limited to recent episodes of my life. It includes all my past of emotions, thoughts and experiences. It also comprises all the past of my ancestors, humankind, the planet and the universe. It is a sense of strong discomfort that makes me feel wrong and inadequate. A typical trait of guilt is that, once I feel it and believe in it, as a result I begin to convince myself that sooner or later I will be punished. Anyone who commits a crime is either arrested or lives with the fear of being arrested. In the same way, once I experience guilt, I unconsciously feel deserving of punishment. The threat of this punishment is the origin of all kinds of *fear*. In brief, if I believe in sin, i.e. that I am separate from God, I move directly from sin to guilt, and from guilt to punishment, to arrive then in fear. As I believe I have sinned against God and have separated from Him, I fear that He is going to punish me for what I suppose I have done to Him.

The cycle of sin, guilt and fear, once in motion, creates a continuous repetition, a sort of vortex from which the ego gets its vital nourishment. It seems as if there is no way out from this tragic situation. Its fear and misery are unbearable and, in order to release them, I need help. The point is that, until I am taken by this vortex, it is not possible to ask God for help. According to the ego system, God is actually the one from whom I need to defend myself. The ego sees God as an enemy and fosters the idea that He is going to punish me for what I have done. In order to find some relief, as long as I am in the vortex, the only way is to open up to the ego. Its availability to rescue me is soon very clear. As a matter of fact, such availability stems from just one need: that of preserving the existence of the ego. The ego is that part of the mind which believes in separation. Therefore the basic work of the ego consists of doing all that is needed to preserve the separation and its cycle of sin, guilt and fear as real. The survival of the ego depends upon this belief. As long as I believe in guilt, the ego can continue to play its games, and all the help that is going to come from within its system will always contribute to support the same guilt from which I wish to be released.

Repression is the first type of aid that the ego offers. It is about taking all the grievances, pushing them down into the unconscious, and then pretending that they are not there. It is the most popular solution, although it usually doesn't last for long. One part of me, even if I am not aware, knows very well that the problem is still there. It is like throwing all the rubbish in a house into a hidden room. For a while it works. Then as the amount of rubbish increases it begins to squash against the door of the room. Its smell starts to permeate outward and then invades the whole house. The same process happens with the guilt which is repressed. To avoid this type of problem the ego provides a more sophisticated tool: *projection*. This involves taking all the guilt I have inside and throwing it on to somebody else. In this way, the guilt which I do not want to see in myself, I will see in them, him or her. It is like tossing my rubbish into the house of a neighbour, and then accusing him of being filthy and stinking. The fact is that projection operates so quickly and secretly that I am really not aware that the rubbish I see in my neighbour's place is indeed mine. Somebody else becomes responsible for the misery, the suffering, the pain that exist in my life. It does not matter who that somebody is. What counts, for the ego, is to manage to find somebody or something on which to unload all that I have inside.

Projection is the most effective method that the ego employs to get rid of guilt. Unfortunately, it is also the best way to keep and exalt it. It is an ego trick to make me feel different from others and to reinforce my belief in separation. Indeed, when I accuse somebody else of being the cause of my pain, at a certain level, I am aware that I am just running away from the responsibility for the guilt that I feel within. Through this dynamic I contribute to a vicious circle of guilt and attack. The more I feel guilty, the stronger the need to deny my guilt and to project it on to somebody else. The more I attack that somebody, the stronger my guilt will be, as I intimately know that my attack is not justified, and that I am only attacking myself.

A very subtle form of projection is called the *special love relationship*. This is a relationship that, although it seems quite different from the previous one, is only the other side of the coin. We have seen how human beings, according to the ego system, cannot ask God for help. This situation creates a state of incompleteness and determines the need to find somebody special with whom to feel good. It is an agreement in which if somebody does something for me, then I love him or her and, as a form of exchange, I can do something for him or her. This is what is usually considered to be *love*: a relationship bound to support the vicious circle of guilt. On one hand, the relationship satisfies my needs and this makes me feel good. On the other, it increases my dependence on the partner and the fear of losing him or her. In the end this awakens the memory of the guilt that unconsciously caused the birth of the relationship itself. As it is the guilt which frightens me more than anything else, and as my partner triggers it again in me, then I am going to attack and hate him or her as well. Due to guilt, all special relationships have fear in them. That is why they change so often. When there is fear in a relationship, there is no space for love and what is left is only guilt.

To sum up, the ego, after having generated the cycle sin – guilt – fear, provides first aids such as repression and projection. These tools actually reinforce the pain that they pretend to heal.

The Function of Forgiveness

The answer to the vicious circle of the ego is *forgiveness*. This term has a different definition from its conventional meaning. Here *to forgive* does not mean to feel superior and tolerate those who harm me. This is again an ego trick aimed at creating separation. To forgive means to correct the idea that somebody did harm me.

It is forgiveness for something that the other never did, not for what was done. 'To forgive is merely to remember only the loving thoughts you gave in the past, and those that were given you. All the rest must be forgotten. Forgiveness is a selective remembering, based not on your selection.' *(ACIM, Text, p. 354)* With forgiveness the same tools employed by the ego to trap me in the world of separation and guilt are used to release me. Through the external projection on people or situations, I have the chance to see the guilt that I have repressed within. It is an opportunity to watch the guilt outside, and then realise that it is inside and that there is no separation within and without. In this context, the most difficult situations of life are indeed decisive times that allow me to see what I could not be able to see in other ways.

The process of forgiveness may be described in three stages. The first is about taking the projection from the outside to the inside. This involves using the opposite process of the ego and acknowledging that the problem is not outside. The problem is inside. The reason why I am unhappy or miserable is my responsibility. If I continue to believe that the responsibility is outside, I will employ my energy outward in search of a solution. The trick of the ego is to confuse me with thousands of apparent problems in order to prevent me from facing the only real problem: i.e. separation. In this way, the ego, going through one unreal problem after another, weaves an intricate web which is meant to support its own insane power.

In the second stage, I accept my responsibility and reinstall the guilt in my mind. I acknowledge that it is within me, I observe it, and I realise that I have made an error of choice. The guilt reveals itself as the result of a decision taken in the past: that of considering myself as a child of the ego instead of a Child of God, a decision related to a very ancient past, that, in the present, I can choose to change. The awareness of the power of choice is a major point. My own mind has created the illusive world that I perceive as real, and only that mind can choose to alter that world of hallucination. I have done my best to build a hell on Earth, a place where ecstasy and joy are just passing dreams. Although the insanity of this world is clear to most sensible minds, the trend to go on holding on to it is equally strong. When I am willing to forgive, to let go of the past, of my insane ideas about life, and to give up the urge for separation, then the ego system begins to subside. Here comes the third stage of forgiveness. It is not up to me to remove guilt. I am trapped by what I have myself created and I need help from another source. Now I am not prey of the illusive rescue of the ego anymore. I have chosen to look for real help and to refuse to accept deluding solutions or to wait for the achievement of a perfection that will never come. In this way I acknowledge that I am ready to receive that help I was afraid to get before: i.e. God's.

God answers with the removal of guilt and the release of all its effects. The old dream dissolves, the virtual reality fades away and reveals what had always been behind it: love, peace, bliss, unity, joy, ecstasy. This is what *A Course in Miracles* means by *miracle*. It does not mean to multiply bread and fish or to walk on the surface of the sea. It means to radically change my perception of reality. 'Therefore, seek not to change the world, but choose to change your mind about the world.' *(ACIM, Text, p. 445)*

Such an operation is a deep transformational process which involves a major uncovering of what I have decided to hide from my awareness. Rather than ignoring grievances and most desperate hidden feelings, trying to dispel them by focusing only on the *positive* or using the will to push them into the unconscious, here I learn to open up to their true nature. Then I begin to feel and accept them for what they are, instead of confining myself to a conventional illusion of well-being, trying to retreat into a deceptive *light* or playing the role of the victim. Astroshamanism is about taking full responsibility for my presence in the material plane, giving up my denials, acknowledging what exists on Earth and patiently undoing separation. True forgiveness and release occurs when I have fully seen and understood what I am letting go of. Those who honestly accept the exploration of their shadows, withdrawing their projections on others and integrating them into the wholeness to which they belong, are offering, as I see it, a most valuable service to this planet.

Sun and Moon

The Moon traditionally represents night, darkness, passivity, instinct, reflection, soul, shadow, secondary attention, Level 2. The Sun represents day, light, activity, reason, creation, spirit, primary attention, Level 1. The lunar cycle describes the phases of relationship between these two celestial bodies as it is seen from the geocentric perspective of the Earth. From that standpoint Moon and Sun both appear to rotate around the Earth, and seem to have the same kind of size. The relationship of Sun and Moon can describe the rapport between Intent and Function. The Intent corresponds here to the Sun as creative will. Focusing on the Sun creates an energy field which allows the power needed to express my Intent and draw it to me. The Moon stores the ancient memories of the process of separation and puts in evidence the repeated cycles of such experiences. The Moon confronts me with the *shadow*, the *demon*, Level 2, the secondary attention, and what has been repressed and denied. As a result it brings me face to face with what needs to be forgiven. As well as connecting with the Intent (Sun), to undo the illusion of separation and return to the awareness of unity, I need to face and heal the different ways in which I perceive objective reality. These parts (Moon) continue to cause grievances until they are fully acknowledged and released. The capacity to balance the symbolic relationship between Sun and Moon determines the quality of life on Earth. For example, I am driving a car and I intend to arrive punctually at a place for an important business appointment (Sun). After a while I find myself stuck in a traffic jam (the objective reality on Earth). In this case my reactions (Moon) can vary. I could get upset, worried, anxious, impatient, angry and furious to the point that I argue, fight or cause damage to myself and others, or I could be detached, relax myself, release my fears, meditate or happily relate with the environment. My Intent as a businessman is that of being punctual, effective and successful. If something happens to me which does not allow this, it is likely to disturb and annoy me. In the same circumstance, I can also choose to pick up another frequency, which in this case could be simply to relax and be patient. I can recognise the Moon as a force that challenges the Sun. The annoying lunar need is to relax and have a nap, whereas the primary aim is to arrive punctually at a meeting. Here there are two energies at work. Life on Earth can be perceived as the constant interaction between Sun and Moon, day and night, Intent and Function. This feature is strategically described by the lunar cycle and the relationship between the zodiacal signs in which Sun and Moon find themselves. For this purpose it can be useful to be aware of these astrological positions and employ them to monitor the energy of the day as they are reflected both within and without.

1 This section is also inspired by the writings of Kenneth Wapnick, founder of the Foundation for A Course in Miracles (see Bibliography).

CHAPTER 4

PRACTICES AND RITUALS

One of the aims of this text is to provide tools to stimulate and develop the experiential aspects of shamanic work. The practices and rituals that you find here are activities based on an Intent connected with the Function that, according to the vision I refer to, is forgiveness and the retrieval of the awareness of our spiritual nature. In astroshamanism I employ healing practices and rituals, both for individual and group use. *Practices* are exercises, games or techniques that do not usually require the presence of a formal context. *Rituals,* on the other hand, take place within a specific outer or inner ceremonial space and include procedures that need to be followed in detail. The techniques described in this text can be employed by anyone who is sincerely interested in developing shamanic potential. It is not necessary to have a teacher to practise these techniques. Yet, in order to facilitate the work, it can at times be useful to receive support from a competent shamanic facilitator or to operate together with other seekers.

Practices and rituals have been used in all ages by different traditions. Much caution is required here, for each tradition employs its own language, whose sound, grammar and form may be distinct from those of others. Rituals are the fundamental means of expression for most spiritual languages. The fact of a language being *spiritual* does not at all imply that the ego is not going to find any space there. On the contrary, the main area of development for the ego and its belief based on separation abides in *spirituality* and in all kinds of religious, metaphysical, and initiatory contexts. It is there, at a very subtle level, that the ego fights its most strenuous and ultimate battles. The decadence of genuine shamanism is inevitable whenever a series of phenomena – such as complex rituals, moral obligations, ordeals and dependence on an authority – begin to prevail. This is just an invitation to be very vigilant whenever you read or hear anything *spiritual* (including this literature and the information I provide) or perform ritual practices. No matter how careful I am, my fragmented perception and biased views are going to affect part of what I write or say. Always trust what you feel to be right for you and confirm it with your authentic spiritual values.

Each one of us contains the energies of all the sectors and regularly expresses them, although this is often done in an unbalanced or unconscious way. Rituals, when not abused or employed for manipulative purposes, allow a direct communication with these energies and enhance their balancing. As a matter of fact, each act of human life, as I see it, is a ritual act. The whole existence on Earth is based on rituals. Some of them convey unity, love, forgiveness, while others are connected with myths of misery, competition, separation, revenge and other grievances. The discrimination point in rituals is the quality of the Intent – the seed of each practice, whether it be a solemn religious ceremony or a simple daily activity – and its connection with the Function. The Intent expresses itself through my mind and the way I think. A rather unpleasant fact, in this context, is that, without being aware of it, many human beings seem to spend most of their time in celebrating rites of separation, hate and misery. Such rites are not those of traditional black magic or Satanism. These are performed by a rather small minority of dark witches or magicians and are trifles when compared to what is regularly done by ordinary people. The latter celebrate rituals of death and separation whenever they nourish their minds with thoughts of guilt, envy, fear, judgement, revenge, attack, competition, etc. The widespread addiction to tools such as television, radio, films, videos and newspapers often tends to further amplify this insane proliferation of thoughts. These thoughts reinforce the belief in an illusory reality where human beings pretend to be victims of what they are indeed creating.

The practices and rituals employed in astroshamanism allow me to experience the power that is always available whenever I decide to open up to the reality of unity. They connect with my most authentic side and with its original Intent. By creating a sacred space and a protective environment, where I am not easily prey to daily fears and madness, these rituals operate as catalysers of experiences of love and unity. These experiences are the result of a sacred relationship that I create with those beings I meet during the rituals (other participants, people, Guides, Spirits, etc.). They are relationships where I give and receive at the same time. In particular, the situations of fear and grievance are of great importance as they point to what needs to be released. The basic purpose of rituals is indeed that of becoming aware of the blocks which are to be relinquished so as to open up to the miracles which lie beyond.

The ideal moments for a ritual are often associated with the conventional rhythms of this planet and solar system (seasons, solar and lunar cycles, planetary transits) and of their inhabitants, communities, tribes and large groups (agreements, birthdays, relationships, deaths, births, anniversaries, national or religious events). The most significant days are usually those of the equinoxes and solstices, mid-seasonal festivals, full or new moons and ingresses of Sun in a sign. Yet, again, the major requirement is always that of having a pure Intent and being willing to connect it with the Function.

The Sacred Circle Pieces

The creation of the sacred space is essential for a ritual. One of the functions of any practice is just that of making myself fully aware of the nature of the space that surrounds me. For this purpose it is not necessary to have large physical spaces. The area of the Sacred Circle, by virtue of its sacredness, becomes representative of immense extensions even when it is confined to a small space.

The *Sacred Circle Pieces* represent the basic equipment for building the Sacred Circle and are also a significant astroshamanic tool of power. To build them you start by getting twelve pieces of stiff card or wood (or twelve stones, crystals or any material that appeals to you) to be used for each sector, or zodiacal sign. Five other pieces of different dimensions are employed for the Four Directions and the Centre. The type of material you use or where it comes from is not important. You can either find it in nature or buy it in a shop. What matters is that you like it and that it *speaks* to your heart or draws your inner attention. If you decide to collect stones or other materials from nature, it is customary and advisable to state your Intent and explain to the Spirit, or shamanic form, of the place what you plan to do with the stones. Then, you can ask permission and wait silently for a sign of confirmation. If you sense that it is all right to take the stone or material as a piece for your Sacred Circle, it is good practice to leave an offering in its place as a sign of respect and love. This can be seeds, nuts, herbs, a hair from your head, or anything that is fitting or can be recycled in nature.

When you have collected all the material you need, you can activate the five pieces for the Four Directions and the Centre. With these you can already create the structure of the Sacred Circle and start your first practices. Then, every time that you work with a zodiacal sign, you are going to activate one of the other twelve pieces. The activation consists of drawing or painting on the card, wood or stone what is related to your intuitions or visions about that sector. You can also simply write down the name, number or symbol of the sign (see Chapter 2, 'Provisional Reference Chart of the Twelve Sectors', page 33), or create collages. If you use stones, they can be painted, carved, left as they are or chosen according to their natural colour. Another possibility is that of using a sheet or carpet on which to draw a circle with twelve spaces for the twelve signs and five for the Four Directions and the Centre. You can either use it to array the Sacred Circle Pieces or draw them on the sheet itself. Let the decision on how to build the pieces come from within. Remember that this is sacred work and it does not necessarily have to please the body's eyes or correspond to artistic standards. The only thing that matters is that what you do is the result of your deep connection with the Sacred Circle.

To make the activation more effective you can proceed in those periods of time that enhance the energy of the sector involved, i.e. at New or Full Moon, planetary hours or days, solstices, equinoxes, etc. There are various methods of activation you can choose. Some are complex, while others are more simple: such as opening the Sacred Circle and stating your Intent and what the piece is going to represent. Whatever you elect to do, it is important not to create complications, unless you really enjoy them, and to remember that the essential requirement is holding a clear Intent.

Once you have activated a piece, sit in front of it, bring your attention to your breath and open up to what comes to you. After calling your Spirit Guide, you can also connect with the Totem Spirit, express gratitude, dance, chant or pray. Do what is spontaneous for you and be aware of what happens. At any moment, whenever you need to relate to a particular sector, you can always position yourself in front of it. It is like visiting a friend. You only need to remember the address and learn the road. The Sacred Circle Pieces serve this function. Once you have completed all of them and experienced a direct connection with each sector, which generally takes one full year, you will possess a powerful tool and will have realised the basic circumference of the Sacred Circle, or *circle on the floor*.

The Circle on the Floor

One of the typical methods of reading in experiential astrology and astroshamanism is the so-called *circle on the floor*. The natal chart is reproduced on the floor in an ample circle where the person can move or pause, experiencing the energy or the characteristics of the sectors. During individual or group sessions the Sacred Circle Pieces are employed to represent the Twelve Sectors and the Four Directions. Additional pieces can at times be used to identify the planets and the houses.

It is not necessary to know astrology to take part in these sessions. The intellectual or cultural understanding of signs and planets is irrelevant to the effective outcome of the work. What counts is instead to be open to contact that part, within us, that has an innate and authentic awareness of these symbols. Usually, only a few moments of silence are enough, and it is amazing how significant emotions and experiences come out and easily take form, without the need of stimulation, descriptions or interpretations. For example, in the position of Mars, or Sector 1, most people feel a great force, connect with their basic drives, find the courage to be themselves, manage to express what they feel, release anger, take initiatives and become self-assertive.

The circle on the floor is a most powerful instrument and it is necessary to access it with respect and responsibility. In particular, it is essential to make sure that each participant can choose when to stop. For example, if in a certain sector a person feels a strong sense of discomfort, he can always return to a more relaxed or convenient position in the chart or move to the Centre of the Sacred Circle. This space represents our centre of awareness, the point that helps us disidentify from the roles and stereotypes of the zodiacal signs. Here I can learn to accept, understand and integrate the different parts of myself, without denying, projecting or repressing them.

Protection

Astroshamanic work is going to touch different parts of your being. Some of them are familiar, others less so, while some can appear quite weird or scary. The exploration of sectors can cause a large variety of reactions. When I journey into other dimensions or move through my ordinary daily life, I meet areas of ecstasy and beauty, as well as zones of grievances and shadows. The latter can often hide important lessons. The advantage of shadow areas is that they keep me away from situations that I am perhaps not ready to face yet. Their disadvantage is that often the fear of the shadow, and not of what is actually there, can prevent me from having access to significant opportunities and breakthrough experiences. Here care is needed not to get trapped in the bargaining, conflict and confusion which the ego tends to use at this stage. It can be good to take risks, but it is also wise not to force myself. Sometimes it is better to stop for a while and find out what is happening. If a situation creates a lot of unease and I do not feel protected, there is really no point in forcing or harming myself. Even the most powerful shaman does not move a single step in an area of danger if he is not sure of receiving the support of his Guide. And it is indeed this capacity of calling for help and moving only when that aid is available, that makes him a powerful shaman.

A first lesson to learn in every spiritual path is that of *protection.* When I leave the world of consensus reality to search for what lies beyond, my physical and emotional bodies often become more vulnerable. This is very threatening to the different ego layers of my personality. They have been programmed to keep me anchored to, and conditioned by, the physical reality and all its magical beliefs. Their release and deprogramming require some time. In this case it can be wise to attribute provisional power to something from the outside. By performing an act of protection (through a ritual or through the employment of specific tools) I prevent the ego mind from precipitating into panic. I also avoid being affected by energies that I am not yet ready to handle and could perceive wrongly due to my state of fear.

There are different ways of asking for and receiving protection. The Spirit Guide and Circle themselves are major devices for protection. They are always there within and without myself. When this is fully acknowledged and experienced, there is no point in asking for their protection. The fact is that untrained human minds are often not aware of this help and, even when they are, they tend to forget. For this reason I suggest using specific procedures for self-protection. At the same time, it is also essential not to get too rigid, dogmatic or dependent about protection, as this would surely have the opposite effect. The form of protection which is used acts only as a container. What counts is whether this container actually includes protection: i.e. if I truly choose to receive protection and release the subtle temptation of wanting to be attacked. The focus on the Intent to accept protection is indeed a basic requirement of any ritual practice.

Calling in the Directions and Opening the Sacred Circle

The procedures for opening the Sacred Circle correspond to the moment when the sacred and spiritual space is acknowledged. The Circle is a living dimension and all its parts have the capacity to interact and relate with us. During a ritual I access my natural talent to connect with these forces. The energy generally proceeds through circular spiral movements. The opening of the Sacred Circle often consists in shaping the energy in the form of a double cone: the *Sacred Cone*. First the four horizontal directions are called (base of the cone) and then the three vertical directions (the apexes of the cones and the centre of the common circle).

Before starting the opening sequence, arrange the objects and, if this resonates with you, do some smudging (see this Chapter, 'Purification and Smudging'). If you wish, you can physically address each direction. Many traditions start from the East, yet this is not mandatory. Clap your hands, stamp your feet, beat a drum or shake a rattle. You can also use a statement such as 'I call upon the Spirit of the East'. Once you have invited the East, move clockwise towards the other directions (South, West, North) until you have covered them all. Then face the Centre and open the vertical axis. Look above and call to the Sky, or Higher World; then put your hands on the ground and call the Earth, or Lower World; finally enter the space of the Centre, that of the Middle World. This opening procedure is already a healing work in itself as it tends to balance possible disharmonies that you have in relation with the four elements and the Three Worlds.

During the opening stage, as in other ritual phases, it can be useful to employ the phrase 'For All My Relationships'. This is a formula used by some indigenous people in North America, that emphasizes the willingness to honour all beings, close or distant, who have had, or continue to have, an influence in our lives. These relationships – together with those of the animal, vegetal and mineral realm – are considered as family ties. We are all part of the same unity and each relationship is a sacred connection of healing and teaching.

The brief invocation, or prayer, that follows is just one of the many possible examples for calling in the directions. There are specific beings and qualities which are associated with each direction and they can be named in an invocation. This does not mean that they are the only beings or qualities. For example, as I am addressing North I could feel that an animal, different from the ones traditionally found in this direction, is drawing my attention. The key here is to give priority to the vision and trust it. By making the calling in of the directions a spiritual expression of my heart, I invite all that resonates to come to me. And this means that I need to be ready to welcome and accept it.

Behold Spirit Circle, Guide, Great Energy of Love and Light That Moves Through All. I call upon the Four Directions, the Twelve Sectors and the Three Worlds.

I call to the Keepers of the East, Direction of Fire, the intuitional and spiritual realm, Spring and its signs Aries, Taurus and Gemini, place of dawn, birth, new beginning, clarity, wisdom, inspiration, illumination and of the predatory animals. Be with me and show your ways.

I summon the Keepers of the South, Direction of Earth, the physical realm, Summer and its signs Cancer, Leo and Virgo, place of high noon, vitality, passion, growth, trust, love and of the peaceful animals of the Earth. Be with me and show your ways.

I turn to the Keepers of the West, Direction of Water, the emotional realm, Autumn and its signs Libra, Scorpio and Sagittarius, place of the evening, release, strength, experience, introspection, and of the reptiles, fish and animals of the sea. Be with me and show your ways.

I invite the Keepers of the North, Direction of Air, the mental realm, Winter and its signs Capricorn, Aquarius and Pisces, place of night, cleansing, renewal, purity and of the birds. Be with me and show your ways.

I raise my hands toward the Sky and call upon the Higher World, the head, the luminous realm of the stars and galaxies. Be with me and show your ways.

I place my hands on the ground and connect with the Lower World, the belly, the dark realm below and all its beings, seen and unseen. Be with me and show your ways.

And I put my hands on the heart, calling upon the Middle World, the Sacred and Spirit Centre, the place where my Spirit Guide, my Intent and Function abide. Be with me and show your ways.

I claim this work to serve in accordance with the Plan of Salvation and my Intent connected with the Function.

If you feel drawn by this model and you do not have one of your own, feel free to employ it in the beginning or change it according to your requirements. Then, after a while, it is preferable to develop your own way of opening the Sacred Circle. Trust yourself and what you receive through your Guide. Please remember again that there is not a *right* way or spell to do this. The best way is to be spontaneous and allow words or sounds to come from your heart.

Many traditions use rattles, drums or other items to call in the directions. Although this can help, the sound or whisper of your voice is also effective and practical. A simple call of 'Welcome', 'Ciao', 'Ho', 'Hi', etc. works. An important point is that of not giving up the practice because of lack of drums, rattles or voice.

When you have completed the ritual or practice for which you have made the calling, it is an act of honour to release the directions. In this context there are again countless possibilities. One way is to reverse the model for calling in the directions, releasing and thanking each direction in the opposite order to that they were called. The releasing statement need not be lengthy.

Oh Spirit Circle, Guide, Great Energy of Love and Light, thank you for giving me protection as I apply my Intent and Function. I release the Four Directions, the Twelve Sectors and the Three Worlds. I claim this work to serve in accordance with the Plan of Salvation and my Intent connected with the Function.

Purification and Smudging

Smudging is a traditional strategic method of purification employed in many rituals. Besides being typical of various shamanic cultures, it is also used in the rituals of most religions. Through this practice, the smoke of herbs or incense is employed to cleanse the energy of people, spaces and objects. Smoke is an etheric substance which can easily move through the different layers of the body. The physical body is surrounded by subtler bodies which are denominated by different traditions with the term *aura*. The aura is an area of constant communication and transit for all kinds of energy. It is regularly influenced by the relationship with inner and outer agents and just as the physical body, gets dirty or is subject to alterations both through its exposure to the environment and as a consequence of internal processes. The agents that affect the subtle bodies have an emotional, mental and spiritual nature. Smudging is a strategy to clean the aura and the surroundings of any thought or emotion that is not in harmony with the purpose of a ritual. It is meant to represent the willingness to release energies that could hamper the work and draw those that are helpful and supportive.

Typical herbs traditionally employed for smudging are various kinds of sage (*artemisia tridentata,* or prairie sage; *salvia apiana,* or white sage; and also *salvia officinalis.* or garden sage) and cedar (*thuja occidentalis, thuja plicata*, *calocedrus descurrens*), lavender (*lavendula officinalis*), copal (*bursera odorate*) and pine (*pinus sylvestris*). Also almost any herb which burns well, smells good or resonates with the user can be used for the purpose. It is preferable to employ plants that grow locally, as this honours the shamanic custom of using what is available in the immediate environment. Remember that it is always your Intent connected with the Function that creates true power. When the Intent is unclear, separated from the Function and related to incongruent hidden agendas or desires, herbs or other ritual implements are useless and can have undesirable results.

A classical smudging procedure that I employ consists of placing a quantity of herbs in a container (a pot or a shell, for instance).[1] After thanking the plant, I focus on my Intent and connect it with the Function. I light the herbs and offer the smoke to the four horizontal directions (East, South, West, North), moving it three times towards each of them. Then I offer it to the three vertical directions, holding it high for the Higher World, setting the smudge on the ground for the Lower World and keeping it in my hand at heart level for the Middle World. Next I cleanse my hands in the smoke by holding the smudge in front of me with one hand, using the other to direct the smoke over my body (alternatively I can use a feather) as follows: four times each toward my heart, my head and belly. I conclude the smudging by drawing the smoke to my heart and allowing my hand to rest on it for a while. The smoke can also be directed to other parts of the body, to objects, people, plants and to the corners of the room.

It is proper to smudge daily or twice a day and whenever needed. Besides smudging there are also other forms of purification like water or sound. A shower, a chant or a drumming can be turned into an act of cleansing if they are performed with this Intent. Each element has specific tools for purification: fans, flags, bells, whistles, feathers, rocking chairs and smoke for Air; sand, stones, ash, crystals, salt, chalk, flour, rice for Earth; water, oil, saliva, blood, urine for Water; candles, torches, pyres, embers, lamps for Fire.

Please be aware. Smudging and other practices that involve the use of external agents to produce purification or healing are forms of *magic*[2] and therefore basically illusory in their outcome. Those materials have no real power to heal as they are part of the *sickness* itself. This again means that the basic factor lies in the Intent connected with the Function. At the same time, employing such magical practices could in certain circumstances be the best solution. 'Sometimes the illness has a sufficiently strong hold over the mind to render a person temporarily inaccessible to the Atonement. In this case it may be wise to utilize a compromise approach to mind and body, in which something from the outside is temporarily given healing belief. This is because the last thing that can help the non-right-minded, or the sick, is an increase in fear. They are already in a fear-weakened state. If they are prematurely exposed to a miracle, they may be precipitated into panic. This is likely to occur when upside-down perception has induced the belief that miracles are frightening' (*ACIM, Text*, p. 24)

The Individual Practice

Astroshamanic practices are operations of strong energetic catalysation that allow the activation, receiving and release of large amounts of information. To support this process and allow it to be grounded in ordinary reality, it is important to set aside some regular time for shamanic work and the exploration of your inner world. For this purpose it may be convenient to identify soon an individual practice that you can employ daily or at least three times per week. It can be in the form of a meditation, shamanic journey, prayer, dance, chanting, etc. As a bare minimum, you can light a candle or incense, use the smudging procedure described in 'Purification and Smudging', open the Sacred Circle, focus on your Intent and Function or go to the Spirit Circle[3] and meet your Guide. It does not matter the type of practice you choose. What counts is that you commit to honour it regularly. This is a sign of your willingness to expand your perception and open up to the relationship with your Spirit Guide. From the very beginning it is useful to find something that appeals to you. 'Always remember,' says Osho, 'whatsoever you enjoy can go deep in you; only that can go deep in you. Enjoying it simply means it fits with you. The rhythm of it falls in tune with you: there is a subtle harmony between you and the method.'[4] Once you find that practice, go into it as much as you can. Avoid being distracted by other methods and stick to the one you have chosen for a minimum of 28 days. Then, if you realise that the practice is no longer a source of inspiration or joy, you can drop it and search for another method. Be aware that 'No method can lead you to the very end. On the journey you will have to change trains many times.'[5] The second book of this work contain exercises that you are invited to try, yet these should not be used as a substitute for your regular individual practice.

The Astroshamanic Basic Ritual of the Sacred Cone

The *Astroshamanic Basic Ritual of the Sacred Cone* is a classical astroshamanic ceremony celebrated individually or with a group. It usually includes three stages which correspond to three specific Sectors of the Sacred Circle. After smudging and calling the directions, the participants focus on their Intent. Then they walk clockwise around the Sacred Circle stopping at a position they feel drawn to. That point is connected with their Intent and allows its energy to intensify. It is generally the sector which is most aligned with the person's will and desires. Astrologically it is often related to the position of the Sun, Ascendant and their rulers. Everyone is invited to go into the strongest expression of their will and desires, focusing on what he wants for himself and others. This means, as for all stages of the ritual, to open up to feelings, images, sounds, words, or to whatever happens, without judging or premeditating. The Intent, once clear, is expressed through gestures, dance, verbal expressions, chants, sounds, a posture of the body or by just staying in silence.

At the end of the first stage, the participants move in an anticlockwise direction. The expression of the Intent is bound to draw the contrasting elements and create the conditions for the second stage: the Function. The participants choose another sector which resonates with the energy that needs to be released. This often corresponds to limits, blocks, imbalances or great unexpressed potentials. Astrologically it is often associated with the Moon, Saturn, Immum Coeli, Descendant, South Node, midpoints or planets in critical situations. The energy of that sector can manifest through feelings, emotions, thoughts, memories, images of people, or through whatever happens in that moment. The energetic expression is as in the previous stage, although it is preferable to act more intensely here.

This second stage represents the crucial phase of the ritual. It is the moment when everyone is invited to contribute the energy for the sacrifice. *Sacrifice* (from the Latin *sacer* ('holy') and *facere* ('make')) means to make holy or perform a sacred action that, in this context, consists of releasing or giving away something to the Spirits. This sacrifice is an offer of grievances. A *grievance,* or *graha,* is any physical, emotional, mental or spiritual uneasiness, including any attitude or situation, even of apparent well-being, that supports the ego and the illusion of separation. Contrary to common belief, here grievances are the most favoured offerings to Spirits or higher realms. In the trade with shamanic reality they represent material of great value. Here, all situations in which we are full of grievances are indeed moments of great power. 'It is there,' says Ur Kuran, 'that you are confronted with a tremendous choice, the decisive choice that you faced since you began to move your first steps in this location... Whether you are aware of it or not, a part of you knows extremely well how valuable grievances are. Thus, when they become available, you instinctively tend to keep or hide them. When you do that, you betray your original calling. It is a foolish act as grievances do not bring any wealth if you keep them for yourself or sell them in the local markets. Their value is acknowledged only when you access the vertical axis and trade in the interdimensional fairs. This only occurs when you refuse to deposit or let them circulate on Earth... The second stage offers you this opportunity. If you succeed in this enterprise, even for an instant, the gratitude of the Spirits will come abundantly to you.'[6]

In the third stage the participants, after moving in a clockwise direction, position themselves in another sector. Here they are invited to receive and surrender to whatever comes to them as a result of their sacrifice. Once I have made the offer to the Spirits, I can open up and receive. The position chosen in these circumstances is often related to the area, or sector, which has most potential energy. For example, it can be the Medium Coeli, an angular planet, the North Node or a planet with *alien* or *mutant* traits.[7] At the end of the ritual, what has been received can be shared with the other participants. Once the ritual is over, it is important to take notes about the experience and the positions of each stage. The *Basic Ritual* can effectively be employed as a regular individual practice. It can also be performed in a sitting or lying position, without any physical movement and as a shamanic journey to the Spirit Circle.[8]

Moving and Staying in the Circle

There are many ways to use the Sacred Circle and they all work equally well. Each model is good as long as it allows connection with a position and movement to other positions in due course. For example, I can move in a clockwise or anticlockwise direction and explore each sector. I can also visit the sectors of every element or those that are in polarity. In this latter case, first I connect with one sector and then move to the opposite position in the Circle. In group sessions, the participants usually sit in a specific Sector. First they spend some minutes in silence and bring awareness to their breath and feelings. Silence allows the group to release the world of chattering or distractions and enter into the sacred space. After a smudging ceremony, the Spirits are called through chants, drumming, prayers, dances or silence. Then a form of *council*, or *ceremonial sharing*, is used where each person in turn receives the total attention of the whole group. This is generally facilitated by handing round a *talking piece*. This tool – which can be a wand, a crystal sphere, a bone, or whatever is appropriate for the group – has the function of identifying the speaker and the catalyser of energy. Everyone gives total attention, without interrupting or commenting, until the piece is handed to somebody else. The speaker first introduces himself giving his ordinary or spiritual name. In some traditions this introduction is always used, even when all the members of the group are familiar with each other. It is a way to acknowledge and honour the presence of Spirits, ancestors or other unseen beings who come to the gathering for the first time. After saying his name, the speaker can express his feelings or ideas, share an experience or vision, chant, dance, play an instrument, make some gestures or remain in silence. What matters is to find the type of expression that best honours your truth as well as that of the Circle. In this context it is the heart which is invited to speak and listen. This involves respecting the sacred space and the attention that is given by the group, and using spontaneous, clear and concise forms of expression.

When the participants sit in the Sacred Circle they tend to express themselves, mainly unconsciously, according to the traits of their specific position. For example, those who stay in Sector 1 (Aries and Mars) may be direct, energetic, brave, self-confident, and at times impulsive or angry. If someone needs a stronger involvement, he can ask to enter the central area of the Circle. This is a way to get a direct support from the Circle. If there is a block, the person in the Centre can turn toward a sector or a participant who strategically represents its dynamic, and interact with him. If the energy of the Circle is strong, it is possible to experience deep healing and transformative processes. The group can easily resonate with the catalyser and allow the healing power of collective release to operate. Here we begin to realise that our problems have the same communal roots and that we can help each other, simply by being transparent and honest. This means bringing our whole self trustingly into the work (including everything: power, wisdom, joys, talents, fears, ignorance, insecurities, and so on) and offering it to be integrated, released and balanced by the larger flow of the Sacred Circle.

Besides group sessions, the Sacred Circle is a major instrument for individual work. You can create your own Circle and walk in its physical space. Please be aware that the physical presence of a Sacred Circle is not at all mandatory in shamanic work. It is possible to move into the Spirit Circle and do the same work in the shamanic, or non-ordinary, reality. To find your position in the Circle, you can turn around it until you feel drawn by a particular Sector. This can be indicated by a vibration in the body, a magnetic attraction, an image, a light, sound or by the simple decision to go to one place. Entering into or connecting with a sector also does not necessarily need the formal structure of the Circle. For example, if I look up to the sky and I see a cloud shaped in a way that reminds me of a bull, this can be an indication that my position is related with Sector 2 (Taurus). Similarly, as I walk I can notice the unexpected presence of an animal, plant, stone, person or situation associated with a sector. Here the circle of my horizon takes over its original role of Sacred Circle and the area where I live and move becomes a geomantic field of wisdom. The same experiences can happen in a dream, when listening to the radio, reading a book or watching a movie. Usually, when there is a strong and true connection, the same associations are repeated through different media or tools. Life is a Sacred Circle and nothing happens by chance. There are no idle thoughts or situations. Everything has meaning and provides information about where I come from, where I am and where I am going. With this work I learn to pay attention and be alert to all that happens within and without me.

Astrodrama

In ancient times drama was a collective healing practice, whereas nowadays its emphasis is mostly based on entertainment, show business and evasion. In contemporary societies there is a tendency to abdicate from the power of acting and leave it in the limited hands of specialised people. The creative performances of an elite of artists, actors and musicians have become consumer items and others outside the elite rarely believe that they can express the same talents. This attitude deprives us of one of the most effective healing tools. *Astrodrama* is a typical technique of experiential astrology. Its aim is to connect directly with the planetary energies and to translate all personal or social events into myths. With astrodrama the natal chart is experienced dramatically and becomes a field of expression where each participant plays and meets the components of his inner world. In this respect there are various techniques inspired by Jacob Moreno's psychodrama, gestalt therapy and ancient practices, like those of the mystery traditions or Sufism. The distinctive element of astrodrama is that it can draw precious information from the natal chart. This helps identifying actors or scripts and also allows the effects of the drama to be followed. Astrodrama stimulates the individual's creative energy, facilitates the release of unconscious parts and the opening of one's centres, especially that of the heart.

'When the heart is open,' writes Jeff Jawer, 'magic happens. When we align ourselves with the cosmos we open and become magical. This is the astrology of our ancestors. It is not limited to the natal chart, but is the remembrance of the unity of our universe. This is the astrology that teaches us that we are each all of the planets, all of the signs. Our individuality is meaningless without these connections. When my concept of Saturn is only that of "my Saturn" I suffer, astrology suffers, and our world slips further into the darkness. The richness of astrology is its universality. Each of the planets has at least two faces for each of us. There is the face we meet at birth which colors our perceptions of reality. But, there is also the essential face, the pure energy of each planet, each perfect, each a divine teacher and friend. Through the connection of ourselves with the essences of the planets we remember this. We help to heal the earth and ourselves. "As above, so below" becomes not the measure of a distant relationship then, but the embodiment of an intimacy with all of life and its beauty.'[9]

One of the major features of astrodrama consists of translating the natal chart into a theatrical representation where as many actors as planets are involved. There are generally three types of roles: *director* (the person whose chart is dramatised), *actors* (who play the planets, or Totem Spirits) and *focaliser* (the teacher, therapist or facilitator). The integration of these roles gives form to an astrodrama or, as Barbara Schermer defines it, a *Living Horoscope*.[10] The basic format of an astrodrama can be as follows:

a. First the participants look at the natal chart which is to be represented, identifying the key elements and issues, including transits.

b. The director then chooses the actors and give them a planetary role to play. He might also ask the actors which roles they want to play.

c. The director, together with the focaliser, defines the Intent of the astrodrama. Here a focus or guideline for the drama is identified. This stage is essential as it determines the structure of the play. The director instructs the actors regarding their roles and provides information about what he wants to be represented.

d. Once the Intent has been declared, the focaliser considers, together with the director, the order in which the actors play the planets. For the astrodrama they can also employ suitable costumes and props.

e. The actors arrange themselves in a circle according to the positions of the planet they play in the director's natal chart. Then they tune in to the related energy.

f. Each actor begins to play his role by briefly introducing himself. After this prologue the astrodrama develops according to the Intent established by the director.

g. The drama ends with a final scene aimed at supporting the director. For example, it could be a loving gathering of the planets around the director, a soft chanting of his name or a series of positive affirmations.

h. A sharing involving all the participants follows.

An astroshamanic version of astrodrama can be practised in the Sacred Circle. The director goes to the Centre, bringing his attention to the Intent. The actors tune in to the role they are enacting and go into a shamanic journey which leads them to the position of their planet. Here they connect with the planetary energy, or the Totem Spirit, of the sector involved and spend some time in order to receive instructions. Then they come back and share what they have received or play in the astrodrama as channeler of their planet.

1 Also note that incense sticks are an alternative option and can be more practical especially when working indoors.

2 *Magic* in this context is the ego's basic *therapeutic* practice which generally consists in healing a problem that exists in the mind (Level 2) through physical agents (Level 1). Grievances are here projected from the split mind, which actually generates them, to material forms, which are the product of that mind itself, and an attempt is made to heal them at the physical level instead of undoing them in the mind. The former attitude consists of using external agents (like physical medications) to produce healing in the body or mind, whereas the latter implies employing the mind itself to manifest external results.

3 A *Spirit Circle* pertains to the non-ordinary, or shamanic reality, and is only perceived beyond the third dimensional level, whereas a *Sacred Circle* is visible on the outer, ordinary, or physical reality. Please be aware that this is merely a linguistic strategy. From a purely astroshamanic perspective there is no authentic difference between the inner, or non-ordinary, and the outer, or ordinary, reality as they are both part of the same unity. This distinction is an educational strategy used to adjust to the perception of separation prevalent in most human cultures and conditioning.

4 Osho, *The Orange Book: the Meditation Techniques of Bhagwan Shree Rajneesh*, Rajneesh Foundation, 1983, p. 8. (This book, which contains a wide range of meditation techniques and precious insights, is out of print and is currently replaced by Osho, *Meditation: The First and Last Freedom,* St. Martin's Press, New York, 1996.)

5 Osho, Ibid.

6 Oral transmissions from Ur Kuran adapted by the author.

7 *Alien* and *mutant* characters are non-ordinary potentials, or shamanic skills, that can be identified by the presence of certain planets in specific points of the chart. The topic is considered in Chapter 10, 'Non-ordinary Traits'.

8 The author has available drumming compact discs or cassettes specifically created to accompany the Astroshamanic Basic Ritual. For information: Franco Santoro, Cluny Hill College, Forres, Scotland. IV36 2RD
Please be aware that in accordance with the *Sacred Cone Circle* tradition the ritual is currently provided for individual use only. Employment of this ritual in work with other people or in any public event requires a specific initiation and training.

9 Jeff Jawer, 'Astrodrama' in Joan McEvers (ed.), *Spiritual, Metaphysical and New Trends in Modern Astrology*, Llewellyn, 1988, p. 145.

10 Barbara Schermer, *Astrology Alive!: Experiential Astrology, Astrodrama and the Healing Arts*, The Aquarian Press, 1989, pp. 68–74.

CHAPTER 5

THE ASTROSHAMANIC VOYAGE

Since immemorial times the shamanic journey has constituted one of the most ancient and widespread methods of spiritual research. With this type of experience shamans, spiritual masters and medicine people have connected with other dimensions to pursue their healing work. In astroshamanism the journeys take place in specific territorial areas represented by the Three Worlds and the Twelve Sectors. The voyage in those spaces may imply covering distances of different length, and dealing with various levels of organisation and preparation. Certain territories are familiar and allied, while others are unknown or dangerous and require a different spirit from that of the ordinary visitor. In these cases it is preferable to acquire an adequate training.

In astroshamanism we explore dimensions where the capacity to visualise, the awareness of our bodies (physical, emotional, mental, spiritual), the adherence to the Intent and the relationship with the Spirit Guide can be compared to physical agility or technical ability in the material world. The preparation includes also the acquisition of information on the geography of the territory where the journey takes place.

Anyone can safely employ shamanic journeys as long as instructions are carefully followed and there are not any serious physical or psychological problems. If you do not feel safe to proceed alone, you can ask for assistance from a competent facilitator or take part in specific workshops. Although this work is based on experience and does not require adherence to a particular belief system, it is important to be aware that it entails dealing with unknown spaces and most powerful forces. Shamanic journeys are not fantasies or exercises of creative visualisation. The situations and the beings met in these experiences are as real as those of ordinary life. Everyone can work with shamanism and treat it in a playful way, giving to this work the meaning that he finds appropriate. At the same time, in order to play with integrity, in this as in other cases, it is necessary to understand and respect the agreements of the game.

As regards shamanic journeys there are various operative modalities which can be employed. According to my experience and that of various seekers and traditions, I consider the following points relevant to support shamanic practices, especially at an early stage. They have particularly been devised for readers with limited or no experience. If you belong to this category, I invite you to consider the next section carefully, and reread it as you proceed in your work. Yet, please also be aware that the following are simply suggestions aimed at providing a basic structure and given in line with my current perception. As such, they are not absolute or binding. You are a largely differentiated individual and, as you go on, you may develop your own approach and find that other conditions are more effective.

Basic Indications for Shamanic Voyages and Explorations of the Sacred Circle

1. During the hours before, and on the day of, the journey, avoid all kinds of psychedelic drugs or alcoholic beverages. The basic assumption here is that human beings already have all the psychoactive chemicals they need and that a shamanic journey is aimed at activating these natural potentials. In the preceding three hours it is also advisable to abstain from heavy or spicy food, dairy products, sugar, soft drinks, coffee, tea and to eat moderately or not at all. As you travel inward, it is necessary to keep a connection with the outer environment. The exploration of shamanic reality,

although it may appear so, is not a truly *out of body* experience. On the contrary it is intimately related to the essence of the physical body. Far from being transcended, the body is perceived according to a deeper perspective which allows its connection with the more subtle imaginative and intuitive levels of your nature. In a shamanic journey, participation is active and all senses are employed. It is important to feel, and not only see, the inner environment and to consider it keeping the point of view of your eyes or the direct perception of your other senses. If you become aware that you are not being present or that you are looking at an image of yourself, come back into your body, keep the perspective which comes from your eyes and be fully aware of the sensory information you receive. Watching an image of yourself is useful if you are deliberately trying to distance yourself from an experience which is too intense. If you wish to take action or allow deep transformative processes to occur, it is usually preferable to take a more involved part.

2. It is helpful to start and end a shamanic journey with a specific sequence of opening and closing (see this Chapter, 'Sequence of Opening and Closing for Shamanic Voyages'). These sequences strategically demarcate the moment of entrance to the shamanic world and, once you end the journey, your return to conventional reality. As such they support the shift from ordinary to shamanic states of consciousness and an easy integration of your non-ordinary experiences with everyday reality. A basic guideline in shamanic work is that of purposefully committing to return to ordinary reality, once the journey is over. Shamanic practices are generally aimed at bringing knowledge and healing in our visible planetary environment. They are not meant to create further evasions or hallucinations. If you employ an audiocassette or CD specifically created for the shamanic journey, you can come back when you hear the closing sequence. This is usually signalled by a pause in the drumming, a series of slower drumbeats, a very rapid drumming and a final series of slow drumbeats. The duration of a journey varies generally from 15 to 40 minutes. In the beginning it is preferable not to exceed these times.

3. To favour concentration and shamanic states of consciousness the drum, rattle or other specific instruments are employed. They are helpful to synchronise the left and

right hemispheres of the brain and reproduce the wave frequencies associated with heightened awareness. The monotonous rhythm of the drum is effective, for it emulates the heart beat of the mother, which is the first sound that the human foetus encounters in its life. This stimulates ancient memories and connects us with a primal awareness that transcends the way we ordinarily perceive reality. Moreover, drumming reduces the interference of the conventional mind, facilitates the production of visions and provides the signal for the closing sequence. For shamanic journeys, a drumming or rattling tape or CD is equally appropriate.[1] You can also use other tracks like waves, gongs or chants. What matters is that their sound be monotonous and repetitive. It is better to avoid melodic or New Age music. This could easily affect or manipulate the development of the experience and disconnect you from your own vision unless you have deliberately decided to be influenced or inspired by a specific type of energy. Please be aware that the fact that there are many auditory tools for shamanic work does not necessarily mean that it is mandatory to use them. You can also do everything in silence or allow whatever sound is audible in your environment to contribute to the effectiveness of your journey. As a matter of fact, drumming is also meant to amplify the awareness of your own heart beat and, if you manage to connect with it at will, this alone can become a most spontaneous and effective focus point for any shamanic work.

4. Before starting a journey it is advisable to get ready and ensure that your environment is comfortable. Make certain that you are in a place where it is not possible for anybody to see, interrupt or disturb you throughout your entire practice. A frequent occurrence for beginners is that just at the start or during the journey, disruptive things happen in the outer environment: the telephone rings, somebody knocks at the door, a dog barks wildly or people outside make a lot of noise. It is helpful to take all necessary precautions in order to avoid possible interferences: for example, informing those who live with you that you do not wish to be disturbed and disengaging your phone. To create the right energy you may turn off the light, put on a candle, surround yourself with Sacred Tools, smudge and open the Sacred Circle. These indications are strategic and are meant to support your practice, not to create complications. If you

do not find them useful, please avoid them. What counts is to keep an attitude of simplicity and use only what resonates deeply within you.

5. Lie down or sit comfortably on the floor or on a chair. Make sure that your spine is straight. Take off tight clothes and shoes. If it is cold, use a blanket. Unless this causes strong resistance or fear, it is highly recommended to journey in a dark environment or, if that is not feasible, to use something to cover your eyes (your arm or a blindfold). Whatever the case, keep your eyes closed during the journey. Connect with your breath and allow it to move in to all parts of your body, relaxing and grounding yourself. Allow your Intent to gently emerge as you breathe. Focus on your Intent. This preliminary time is essential as it allows clarification of your true motivation. It can find expression through a question, an affirmation, a posture of the body, some ritual gestures, chants or words. The Intent can be an objective in your life that you are aware of and that you wish to receive support or guidance for. Your purpose could be, for instance, that of having a harmonious relationship with a partner or relative, expressing your artistic talent, creating a spiritual community, living in a house in the countryside or achieving any specific result which is authentic and clear. Be honest about your motivations and do not judge them according to the conventional standards of what is right or wrong, spiritual or non-spiritual. Your Intent does not necessarily have to take the form of an achievement which is clear to you. It may also be that of getting to know what your major purpose or potential is, either in this current time of your life or in general. In this case it can be expressed as a question which can simply be: 'What is my Intent?'. The Intent is a time of power when you affirm your determination to know and be available for guidance. Define your Intent with an attitude of respect, not of submission. By clarifying your motivations, you create a magnetic field of energy that draws the forces that you most need in that specific moment. The Intent provides the foundation for your shamanic work and represents a major source of protection in itself.

6. Once the Intent has been established and expressed, you can allow your vision to unfold. Be open and let go of any prejudice or expectation. It is necessary to trust your Guide or any definition of Spirit that you feel connected to, and to

cultivate the certitude that you will get an answer. Here it is not a question of toiling to reach your goal. It is about defining with clarity your Intent, and then allowing the desired answer and the related shamanic experience to develop. This means keeping an attitude of balance between an active and a receptive approach. On the one hand you are aware of your goal and keep an eye on the track, while on the other you follow the stream of energy and open up to its development. The moment that follows the statement, or activation, of your Intent is a key time. Keep relaxed yet attentive and be alert for what comes, as it often follows in a manner that may be unusual for the mind. At the same time, avoid being rigid or becoming too serious. If you lose concentration or your mind wanders, bring back your attention to your Intent, focusing on the rhythm of the drum or any other sound which you have decided to employ and adhere to the structure of your journey.

7. In shamanic journeys it is important to use two basic attitudes. The first is that of holding and employing a specific structure, which in itself is pre-arranged and predictable, whereas the second is of opening to receive and acknowledge what is unexpected and unknown. Journeys in non-ordinary realities are not very different from those in everyday reality. For example, if I wish to go from Edinburgh to London, I can choose various means of transportation (train, car, plane) and different itineraries. According to my choice there are a series of procedures that need to be followed in order to safely arrive to my destination. If I use the car, I need to fill the tank, turn on the engine, drive according to the highway code, follow a specific route, be aware of the likely weather conditions, etc. Similarly, in shamanic journeys, I need to be clear regarding my travel's modalities and comply with them. If I lack this awareness, I risk getting stuck at my departure point, going somewhere else or having troubles during the journey. If my objective is to meet the Spirit Guide for the first time, various procedures are possible. One of them is described in Chapter 6 ('Meeting Your Spirit Guide'). If you decide to use it, simply follow those indications. Once you are clear about the procedures, you can shift to the second type of attitude which involves opening to the journey. While the first attitude requires a precise structure, the second entails opening up to what you meet and experience (landscape, situations, climate, entities, Guides, Spirits, etc.).

8. Any attempt to analyse, judge or rationally explain what is happening during the journey may cause the distortion or blocking of shamanic experiences. Preconceptions and judgements are only an obstacle in this work. If you feel confused, bring your attention to your body. If the mind interferes and you start to intellectualise, or if you receive thoughts and images which are not related to the journey, you can acknowledge them by saying: 'Yes, I have heard you' and instead of trapping them in the mind, allow them to be released. Let them fade into the background and then continue your journey. Avoid getting upset in these instances and try and use your creativity to find expressions that help you circumvent the interference and use them to your advantage (example: 'Thank you for coming. At the moment I am busy. Once I am finished, I will deal with you.') When you have a powerful vision, and you hear a voice in the mind whispering 'You're making this all up', try and reply with 'Making it all up from *where*?' and, if what happens serves you, feel free to continue *making it up*.[2] It is normal for the conventional mind to consider these experiences as inventions and ridicule or disregard them. In these instances a shaman would ask: 'Was it effective? Did it work? Did it heal anything in you or others?' and if the reply is positive, he would add: 'Then, what's wrong with making it up?'.

9. For some people it is at times difficult to see anything during the journeys. Although in our culture sight has acquired a privileged role, it is important to remember that there are also other senses. If you do not see anything, avoid straining your sight and rather use hearing, smell, taste and the feelings of your body. Your visual channel will open up as long as you give space to those senses which are more active in your system. Often in a journey *nothing happens* simply because I have expectations regarding what should happen and I am not available to accept what is indeed happening. In these cases confusion, frustration or loss of concentration soon arise. If attention falls short, bring it back to the last moment when it was present. Do not blame yourself when you are distracted and avoid any judgement regarding the quality of your shamanic experiences, for in this way you are surely bound to interrupt them. In this work, patience is an essential operative requirement. This means allowing the experience to develop spontaneously instead of controlling

it. When you are worried because nothing seems to happen, use some words of power, a sacred chant or the statement of your Intent. Trust the process and your spontaneous way of moving in non-ordinary realities. Be aware of your unexpected perceptions. These perceptions often come at the beginning of a journey and intermittently as you proceed. They are usually hidden because they are cast out by the thought that they are futile, senseless or invented.

10. In shamanic realities customs and situations can be quite different from those of the reality to which you are familiar. As you explore your shamanic world you start to develop the foundations of a new language. It is important to pay attention to messages, signs, images, sensations, no matter how weird or silly they appear. In the beginning, perhaps, you will not understand much, then as you progress in your work and take note of what happens, you are probably going to be amazed by your discoveries.

11. The journey is made together with your Spirit Guide (see Chapter 6). His function is to guide you along the unknown territories of shamanic realities, acting as interpreter, protector and advisor. It is advisable not to go alone on a journey, as this may be dangerous. Once you have found your Guide, it is not possible to lose him. The Guide is always present. The basic point is to call for him and give him permission to be with you so that you can be strategically aware of his presence. Sometimes, especially in the first stages of your journey, the resistance of the ego creates blocks in the form of darkness, fog, monsters or images of people that you know. It is better to disregard whatever you meet before you contact the Guide. Once you have established the connection, your journey can safely start. If you feel confused or do not know what is happening, you can ask for explanations from your Guide. In all circumstances relate and stay connected with your Guide.

12. Sometimes during the journey it may seem that the Guide or the entities you meet remain in silence, refuse to respond to your questions or disappear. This is often an indication that the ego is activating its blocks to manipulate what the Guide is communicating. In these cases, instead of making assumptions about what that silence or disappearance means, it is preferable to insist and give direct permission to the Guide to be there. The act of giving permission and your

insistence allows the defence system of the ego to be circumvented and creates the conditions for the dialogue with the Guide. It is usually the case that true Guides do not interfere with your experience and do not provide information unless you make a direct request. The true Guide also does not judge and abstains from forecasting future events or impressing you with *high-tech* psychic effects.

13. During your journeys avoid working with or on people that you know unless you have received their direct permission in ordinary life. If someone you know appears to you, ask that he takes on the form he has in your shamanic world. At this stage, for example, your friend, husband, wife or father could, for instance, shapeshift into a horse, knight, princess, dragon or crocodile. Then consider that shamanic form together with your Guide and refuse to interact with the physical form of the person involved. Try and use this approach also when the theme of your Intent concerns relations with another person.

14. Immediately after the journey write down notes about the major moments of your experience. The act of recording this information is in itself a powerful practice as it allows the relationship with your shamanic world to be legitimised. Having a record of your shamanic work also makes the information available for future evaluations. When you realise that you have received significant teachings or guidance, find a way to manifest them in your daily life. By giving value to your first journeys, you demonstrate the maturity for further and deeper experiences.

15. Shamanic journeys are part of your most intimate essence and, as a consequence, they belong to a dimension which is hardly understandable according to the conventions of ordinary life. Therefore it is vital to share shamanic experiences only with people that can appreciate and understand them. This attitude allows respect and reinforcement of your sacred space as well as that of the people you meet in your life. Confidentiality regarding the experiences of others is also obviously recommended.

16. When you receive information and advice on your shamanic journeys, these are not to be accepted blindly. True Guides always give good advice, yet it can often happen that the

original message is misunderstood or that you receive directions from *false guides*. It is important to be careful and ascertain that each message is well founded. Avoid surrendering yourself to the guidance you receive and do not worship the Spirit Guide as a god. Test his advice and do not act on it if you suspect that it may not fit with your highest Intent.

17. Moments of resistance, fear, confusion, crisis, grievances or weirdness are an integral part of any deep transformational process. Be aware of what you experience, yet avoid judging your feelings, identifying with them or making interpretations. The expansion of your awareness constitutes a serious threat for the ego and all the fixed ideas you have of yourself. A key point here is to have the courage to sense resistance or fear, pass through them and then take a leap towards the blessings that wait for you beyond the threshold. Situations of apparent grievances may become moments of maximum power that allow you to focus your Intent and reinforce a choice of peace and well-being.

18. Be aware of your results in your journeys. If, after various attempts, you still experience strong difficulties, ask yourself what could go wrong if you succeeded. Carefully consider this question even if you are certain that you want to get positive results. Some people believe they are not entitled to journey in shamanic realities or feel guilty because this is something that they perceive as forbidden. Others fear loss of control or that they may give up major securities in their life. It is important to be aware of conditioning and disturbing beliefs. If you realise that they are still an inherent and valuable part of your vision of life, then it is preferable not to have any shamanic journeys. If this is not the case, it is a question of acknowledging that their time is due and, with this awareness, go back to work with confidence. Another useful option, when faced with difficulties is to take part in specific workshops on the topic or to have individual sessions with a qualified shamanic facilitator.[3]

Sequence of Opening and Closing for Shamanic Voyages

There are different ways to open or close a shamanic voyage. They change according to individuals and traditions. As such none of them is wrong or right. What matters is whether they work and serve the purpose. These sequences are fundamental at the beginning, as they demarcate your entry in and out of your shamanic world. By becoming familiar with such practices, you train your mind so that you can easily shift your state of consciousness. One of the best known sequences works as follows. After you have prepared the environment in which to work, close your eyes or cover them with your left arm or a bandana. Then visualise the entrance to a cavern, any opening into the Earth, gate or door that you remember from some time in your life. When the drumming starts, move through the entrance and proceed along a tunnel until you reach another opening that will lead to the non-ordinary reality. The closing sequence involves leaving the place you have reached in the non-ordinary reality and moving back to the point where you started the journey. This procedure follows the model taught by the anthropologist Michael Harner and is inspired by the tradition of the Jivaro (Ecuador). Other methods, equally effective, involve different postures or procedures. The anthropologist Felicitas Goodman, for example, has studied and practised more than 50 varieties of these postures (see Chapter 9, 'Shamanic Trance Postures').

The following is one of the traditional astroshamanic beginner's procedures for opening and closing a shamanic journey. I offer it as a suggestion and you are welcome to employ it during the first stages of your work. In case it does not suit you, feel free to use your own sequence.

1. Before you start, make sure that you have read and understood the information found in the preceding section 'Basic Indications for Shamanic Journeys and Explorations of the Sacred Circle'. If you wish, you can open the Sacred Circle (see Chapter 4, 'Calling in the Directions and Opening the Sacred Circle'). If you have your Sacred Circle Pieces, you can stay near the piece corresponding to the East or the sector of your Ascendant.

2. Apply point 5 and 6 in the 'Basic Indications for Shamanic Journeys and Explorations of the Sacred Circle'.

3. Relax for some time, focusing on your breath and body. When you are ready, start a drumming tape, if you have one, and feel or imagine a real place on Earth where you can see an entrance. It can be a place where you have been once in your life, a familiar spot or even a place that you have seen in a movie or photograph. As shamanic journeys start from ordinary reality, it is preferable that the departing point be a place existing on this planet. This can be, for example, a door, the entrance to a cave, a bridge, a hole in the ground, a lake, a pool of water, a passage between two trees. What counts is that you feel comfortable with it. Once you have found it, focus on the entrance and take your time to see and sense it clearly in all its details. Then step inside.
4. When you are inside, bring your attention to what you perceive of the place: temperature, colours, smell, sounds, etc. Employ all your senses to discover the environment you are in. Try and understand whether the place is warm, cold, damp, dry. Feel your feet and the weight of your body. Bring your attention to the type of floor and be aware of the air, colours, sounds and any other impressions that you can gather from the place.
5. Continue to move until you find a point of light or opening at the end that will take you outside into another environment or landscape. If you meet obstacles or blocks, move around or pass through them. Finding this entrance is easy and will not require much time. Once you have found it, in the next journeys you do not need to look for it anymore. You simply go the same way as before.
6. Go through this entrance and observe the landscape around you using all your senses. Listen attentively to the sounds that are there, feel the ground underneath your feet, sense the air and the smells, watch whatever you can perceive and be as present as possible. Then after some time, somewhere near you, see a short path leading to a circular area with twelve stones placed around a *Great Tree*. Beyond the circle of the twelve stones there is a border area indicated by four bigger stones representing the Four Directions. This whole area is your Spirit Circle.[4] It is a place where you can go whenever you need energy or protection. Its importance is tantamount to that of your home or room in ordinary life. In your Spirit Circle, you can take rest, feel safe, do spiritual work, balance your energies, meet your Spirit Guide, connect with Totem

Figure 3: The Great Tree

Spirits and other beings. This place is also the starting point of all your explorations of non-ordinary reality. It is like a station or airport which allows connection with all possible directions and times of this world or of any other possible world or dimension. It operates as an area for rebalancing or decompression aimed at facilitating the movement from one dimension to another. The twelve stones that are arrayed around the Great Tree represent the access to each of the Twelve Sectors of the Spirit Circle. From there, once you connect with the Guide, you can move to explore specific areas of the inner world.

7. Once you are fully aware of your Spirit Circle, approach the Great Tree at the centre and look around acknowledging all the stones and whatever you can see. Be aware of what you feel and allow yourself to be totally at ease. Give permission to the Great Tree to balance your energy and release grievances or anything that prevents you from experiencing a sense of peace or power. Receive energy, love, support and all you need from the Great Tree. Sit down by it or hug it. Open yourself to its nourishment and experience a total connection with the sacred environment that you are in. Then the next steps will be those of calling your Spirit Guide and exploring a specific sector. We will deal with these developments in the next chapters. As for now, find your way to say goodbye and employ the closing sequence.

The closing sequence is faster than the opening one. Leave the Circle by following the same route, in reverse order, until you come back to the first entrance. In the drumming tape, the closing sequence is often indicated by a change of beats (for example, three groups of seven slow beats, a very fast drumming, and three groups of seven slow beats again). If you are not employing a tape, set the time of conclusion using an alarm clock, preferably one with a gentle sound, or let your intuition signal when to return.

After the journey, adjust and stretch your body, breathe deeply and gradually come back to ordinary reality. Always jot down what you experienced in your astroshamanic journal. Do that as soon as you finish and avoid leaving it in the belief that you are going to remember everything later.

The Astroshamanic Journal

The astroshamanic journal is a Sacred Tool which allows you to create a bridge between shamanic and ordinary states of consciousness. The act of using the journal is in itself a powerful shamanic practice as it supports the acknowledgement of non-ordinary realities and the development of a field of resonance aimed at amplifying the essence of your spiritual journey. In the journal you collect reports or drawings of your voyages, dreams, insights, visions, life experiences, images, symbols, quotations, notes, and whatever can be useful for your spiritual work. In this way you preserve information that can easily be lost or forgotten. The spaces of the spiritual world do not generally receive the same attention as those of the physical world. A lot of records are available as regards the geography of the ordinary reality. To visit areas existing in the physical reality, information already available is used. To find one's way in a town like Rome, there are maps and signs easily available. There is no point in drawing a map, as this complex work has already been done. On the contrary, for your shamanic geography, you are the one who has to do the exploration and the mapping.

1 Drumming or rattling musical aids created for shamanic journeys can be purchased in specialised record shops. The author also has available drumming compact discs and cassettes specifically produced to provide support for astroshamanic voyages. For information: Franco Santoro, Cluny Hill College, Forres, Scotland. IV36 2RD

2 Edwin C. Steinbrecher, *The Inner Guide Meditation: A Spiritual Technology for the 21st Century*, Samuel Weiser, 1988, p. 73.

3 A session with a qualified shamanic facilitator can allow the connection with your Guide and non-ordinary realities to be amplified and more available to your awareness. It may also give the possibility of releasing blocks, or grievances, that cause difficulties with shamanic perception. In astroshamanism, I tend to work with a cycle of three individual sessions aimed at establishing, supporting and grounding the relationship with the Guide and the discoveries of specific potentials.

4 As mentioned before, the Spirit Circle pertains to the shamanic state of consciousness and is different in nature from a Sacred Circle which is visible to the body's eyes (that is a circle that you arrange with your Sacred Circle Pieces or any stone circle, medicine wheel, etc. that belongs to the physical or ordinary environment). Please also be aware that the Great Tree mentioned in this text is a *Spirit Tree*.

CHAPTER 6

THE SPIRIT GUIDE

Astroshamanic work is based on the connection with the Spirit Guide and Circle. This, far from being accessible only to psychic or visionary people, is an experience available to anyone who sincerely wants it. It is not a difficult task, for this connection has always existed in life and it is only a question of becoming aware of it, remembering how it works and rediscovering its keys of identification. The most difficult side of this relationship is indeed its simplicity. 'We live in a world which teaches us that for a thing to have value it should be difficult to achieve and take a long time to accomplish. [...] The Guide waits for each of us, sometimes throughout an entire life-time. Our collective belief that the outer material plane has more reality than the inner planes blocks our contact with our personal Guide figures. The Guides are so easy to get to that we've forgotten how. In the distant past the relationship to one's Inner Guide was probably so taken for granted that no one ever thought to write down how simple it is to do it.'[1]

The ways to understand the Spirit Guide and Circle, by whatever names they are known, change according to belief systems and spiritual lineage. Although the terminology and the description may differ, the practical effects of the experience are always the same. The terms *Spirit Guide* and *Spirit Circle* are synonyms that depict qualities such as unity, unconditional love, ecstasy, light, joy, or whatever is related to the Divine, or Prime Creator. Although their essential meaning is the same, their different expressions serve to cover two prevalent models common in the imagery of most human spiritual cultures. In this context, the Spirit Circle refers to a collective and territorial unit (*Spirit People* or *Land, Heaven, Ecstatic Dimension,* etc.) whereas the Spirit Guide may be described as the main representative, or prime emanation of, the Spirit Circle (*Spirit Teacher, Master, Inner Guide, Prime Guide, Guardian Angel, Holy Spirit, God,* etc.). If the aim is that of truly connecting, and not of going into theological or philosophical speculations, what indeed counts is to open up to the most effective form of communication which you have personally experienced so far with the Divine and all related qualities, and work on it.

From a limited psychological view, the Spirit Guide may represent the positive qualities that have been separated, or repressed in the conscious mind, during the personal history of a subject. The integration takes place here through the retrieval of such unconscious components and the analytical confrontation with the object on which they are projected. Another approach considers Guides as detached from the personal history of the individual and corresponding to archetypal figures of the collective unconscious. In his *Memories, Dreams, Reflections*, Jung describes this type of relationship when he refers to one of his Guides, Philemone. 'In my fantasies I held conversations with him, and he said things which I had not consciously thought. For I observed clearly that it was he who spoke, not I. [...] At times he seemed to me quite real, as if he were a living personality. I went walking up and down the garden with him, and to me he was what the Indians call a guru.'[2] This way of looking at Guides, outlined by Jung and defined in more detail by other researchers, such as Edwin C. Steinbrecher, shows how it is possible to access one's inner wisdom in a direct way and without becoming dependent on external authorities.

In spiritualism and occultism, according to various mediums, such as Edgar Cayce, Guides are regarded as beings who, after living for a long time on Earth, have accepted the role of helpers for humanity. This help is usually considered as part of their own spiritual journey. As a result, the relationship between human beings and Guides is, in this case, meant to produce positive effects on both sides. According to many occult and spiritualist traditions, it is possible to relate with more than one Guide: some of them have specific functions, while others appear from time to time or during a given period. Only one of them, however, remains at his place throughout all the life of an individual. This is often called the *Guardian Angel,* or *Deva*. It can be described as a permanent Guide that operates as the linking agent between the material reality and the spiritual world. This Guide overviews the relationships with other Guides or Spirits. In the recent developments of spiritualism, such as *channelling* and *contactism,* Guides, as they often tend to point out, express themselves through languages, messages and images that appear different only because they adapt to the level of awareness of the receiver.

In *A Course in Miracles* the Spirit Guide is identified with the *Holy Spirit.* He is described as 'God's answer to the ego' with 'the task of undoing what the ego has made' (*ACIM, Text,* p. 79) or as the Christ Mind which is aware of the knowledge that lies beyond perception. The Holy Spirit is considered as a sort of bridge between illusion and reality, or fear and love. It is 'the part of the mind that lies between the ego and the spirit, mediating between them always in favor of the spirit' (*ACIM, Text,* p. 132), a transformative force that operates within our consciousness to guide us toward an ecstatic perception of life. 'You have set up this strange situation so that it is impossible to escape from it without a Guide Who *does* know what your reality is. The purpose of this Guide is merely to remind you of what you want. He is not attempting to force an alien will upon you. He is merely making every possible effort, within the limits you impose on Him, to re-establish your own will in your awareness.' (*ACIM, Text,* p. 160) He came into being with the separation in order to inspire the *Atonement,* which according to *A Course in Miracles* is the *Plan of Salvation* or correction aimed at undoing the ego and healing the belief in separation so as to fully uncover the true universal experience of union and love. 'Salvation is undoing in the sense that it does nothing, failing to support the world of dreams and malice. Thus it lets illusions go. By not supporting them, it merely lets them quietly go down to dust.' (*ACIM, Workbook,* p. 407) The Holy Spirit is motivated by this Plan, whatever the form or the ways He uses to achieve it. The list of the denominations and appearances that He has used throughout the history of the universe is never-ending. His Function has however always been the same.

The experience of Guides is one of the most typical features of shamanism. Their presence is essential, for they provide a sense of security and protection which is a basic necessity in order to move beyond the borders of ordinary reality. The Spirit Guide operates as bridge between dimensions and is a constant source of balance in all shamanic enterprises. In situations of weakness he is able to stimulate and generate the required power. Yet, whenever you are decoyed by the illusion of separation, he can also be the cause of frustration, pain and despair. For your true nature, the Guide is the deepest companion; just as for the ego, he is the fiercest enemy. Without a direct connection with the Guide, life becomes a forlorn search for altered states of consciousness through the addiction to relationships, sex, work, food, entertainment, drugs and God knows what else.

According to astroshamanism there are different strategic typologies of Guides, or *Sadoha,* as they are called in the *Epic*. The first distinction is that between *Vertical Guides* and *Horizontal Guides*. The former are three and act as the main, basic Guides. Each one of them is associated with one of the Three Worlds (Higher, Lower, Middle). The one to whom I generally refer as the *Spirit Guide* in this text is the *Spirit Guide of the Middle World,* or *Prime Guide,* who can be compared with the Guardian Angel. The connection with him is a basic requirement, as with his help and assistance it is possible to do most healing shamanic work. Horizontal Guides, or *Auxiliary Guides,* are specialised entities that correspond to the Four Directions, the Twelve Sectors and to further subdivisions of the Sacred Circle. Their task is to support us in specific areas and to provide assistance in the development of particular talents. These Guides often appear at the start of the exploration of a sector to accompany us to the point where the Totem Spirit abides. Other differences in Guides are related to nature, age or aspect. They can use forms connected with the human, animal, vegetal and mineral kingdom, employ bodies of beings that are not seen by ordinary human eyes (angels, fairies, mythical beasts, etc.) or even take other less conventional forms (for example: refrigerators, traffic lights, washing machines, vacuum-cleaners, trains). *Bhi Jinah* are other relevant beings of the *Epic*. Their function is to fill the gaps that exist in the physical reality which is perceived by ordinary human beings. The conventional perception supports the hallucination of separation, as physical forms are seen as independent units. Bhi Jinah draw the attention to the linking space that exists between all forms and which the conditioning system of ordinary humankind refuses to accept. Their work is meant to gradually reveal what lies beyond the limitations of ordinary perception. In astroshamanism Spirit Guides are part of the Spirit Circle. The latter comprises the spiritual essence of whatever and whoever is perceivable in a visible physical form. The Spirit Circle also encompasses the concept of Spirit People, or *Etnai,* and also their *Land,* or multi-dimensional geographical location.

According to Edwin Steinbrecher a strategic portrait of the Guide can be drawn astrologically by shifting the Ascendant of the natal chart to the ninth house. The cusp of the ninth house (after the Koch's house system) seems to identify the Ascendant of the Guide, i.e. his appearance and main distinctive features, especially as they are perceived in the first stages of the relationship. Through this perspective other information can be gathered, as all the planets are going to be in specific houses. To intensify the experience of the Guide, a useful place to sit in the Sacred Circle is that of the sector of the ninth house and the house where the Sun of the Guide is. Be aware that this is only a strategic device and is not meant to prevail over the actual shamanic experience. The third house can relate with false guides. This does not imply that it has a *negative* energy. On the contrary, it can offer the precious function of providing the shadow aspect of the Guide and allowing it to be integrated and healed. Also the position of the Lunar Nodes[3] can give further clues and insights regarding the basic features of the Spirit Guide and the false guide.

Meeting Your Spirit Guide

When you get ready to meet your Spirit Guide for the first time, it is important not to create complications with feelings of unworthiness or other thoughts of disempowerment. Always remember that in order to contact your Guide you do not need to be in a state of purity or achieve a condition of immaculate high spiritual vibration. If you were in such states, you would not need to connect with your Spirit Guide. Many people give up the relationship with the Guide because they do not feel in a good mood or believe they do not deserve the connection due to something *bad* they have done. On the contrary, this is often one of the best states in which to relate with the Spirit Guide. The nature of the relationship that takes place with the Guides is an exchange between equals. On one hand I let go of my excess energies, which are welcomed and transformed by the Guide, while on the other I receive the resources I lack and that are abundant in the Guide. The act of releasing my grievances in the presence of the Guide creates the vacuum that allows me to receive. A basic prerequisite for your first meeting is to let go of all your preconceptions, stick to your Intent of contacting your

Guide and employ a technique for this purpose. The Guide can be approached through a wide variety of practices: meditation, shamanic journeys, chant, dance, dreams, etc. In the beginning, to avoid confusion, it is preferable to use a specific procedure. The example that follows is aimed at providing a model for those who contact the Guide for the first time. This procedure is based on the astroshamanic work of exploration of the Twelve Sectors and is simply one possibility among several. In order for the meeting with your Guide to occur, you need only follow the steps and be willing to experience what happens.

1. Start by using the sequence described in the points from 1 to 7 in Chapter 5, 'Sequence of Opening and Closing for Shamanic Voyages'.

2. Once you are in the Spirit Circle, go to the Great Tree and call your Guide. Focus on the Intent to meet him and allow the connection to take place. If you are distracted and do not see the Spirit Circle anymore, go back to the moment when you saw it for the last time and start again from there. If you firmly call your Guide and give him permission to contact you, you are certainly going to see or perceive him in some way. Often you can find him just next to the Great Tree. The Guide can appear in different forms (as a person, animal, light, plant, sphere of energy, voice, sound, and also as body sensations). Receive the first image or feeling that comes to you. If you meet difficulties and do not see or feel anything, state again your Intent of connecting with the Guide and open up without making judgements. If you are not comfortable with what you see or feel, ask the Guide to come in another form. You can also meet a spirit animal that will lead you to the point where you can find your Guide.

3. When you meet your Guide, watch him and receive impressions about his appearance or energy. If you cannot see his face or other details, do not strain yourself. Often, in the beginning, the face of the Guide is hardly visible. Ask him if he is your Guide and if he has the power to protect and support you in your shamanic journeys and spiritual path. Usually, after such a direct request, a true Guide will reply positively either with words and gestures or through any other signal of loving consent. The Guide is also identifiable because he causes strong feelings of unconditional love, protection and support. If you do not feel total acceptance and love, you are probably with a false guide. If you do not receive a

confirmation that you are in the presence of your Guide, focus again on your Intent and give direct permission to your Guide to be perceived by you. Make a clear invitation and open up to receiving your Guide. According to certain traditions, a Guide is also acknowledged as authentic when he is seen at least three times during the same journey.

4. Once you have received the confirmation that you are with your Guide, establish a connection and give him permission to express the love he feels for you. For example, you can ask him to take both your hands in his or to hug you. Stay open to a direct energetic connection and use all your senses to experience it.
5. Get to know your Guide and ask his name. This name is going to be the first that comes to you. Accept it as it arrives to you, even if it sounds unusual or weird. Remember the name so that on the next meeting, you can simply use it to call him. If you do not manage to catch the name of your Guide, identify a mutual recognition sign (for example, a gesture with the hands) that you can employ on future meetings.
6. When you hear the call back (if you are not employing a tape for shamanic journeys, use a gentle alarm clock or let your intuition signal when to return) conclude your meeting. Find your way to thank the Guide, say goodbye and use the sequence of closing given in Chapter 5 ('Sequence of Opening and Closing for Shamanic Voyages').
7. Take three deep breaths, then gradually return to the full awareness of your body and your environment. Jot down the major details of your experience.

During the following days continue to relate with your Guide. Once you have established the first connection it is a question of keeping it alive and deepening the relationship. It is useful to practise this meeting with the Guide regularly (daily or every other day) for a minimum of 28 days. This is the approximate time the Moon takes to move throughout all the signs of the Zodiac and allows a balanced distribution or activation of energy. During the first two or three meetings it is preferable to have simply a silent, loving and energetic contact with your Guide. For example, you can place your right hand in his left hand and allow him to receive your excess energies. Then you can put your left hand in his right and open up to receive from your Guide. Once you have acquired an intimate familiarity with him, and this usually needs at least three meetings, you can ask questions which are relevant for you and your life. Yet, every time you meet the Guide, before addressing questions and receiving the answers, still continue to devote some minutes to establish an energetic connection. Finally, be aware that this relationship needs time to be grounded and grow in your awareness. The ordinary reality and its major belief systems tend to ignore, ridicule or oppose such a connection. For this reason it is preferable to keep the information about your Guide to yourself.

False Guides

In this introductory stage the aim is to ground the relationship with the Guide. One important part of the work here is to discriminate between Spirit Guides and *false guides*. The latter are ego expressions and can easily be identified through the test of love and acceptance. A false guide is unable to give unconditional love and cannot fully accept you for what you are. If you do not feel love, acceptance, peace, joy and the like, with your Guide, this means that you are dealing with a false guide or with some other kind of being that you have taken for your Guide. There are many beings in the shamanic realities and, as they are all quite out of the ordinary and powerful for the layman, it is common to make mistakes. Whenever you do not feel clear, be direct and ask: 'Are you my Guide?' If the answer is positive, allow the Guide to show his love for you. If the answer is negative, or the being you have taken to be your Guide suddenly disappears, tries to distract you with another topic of conversation, does something glamorous or high-tech to exhibit his power or behaves in a way that makes you feel judged, rejected, manipulated or tricked, well, this is a false guide. If this occurs, there is nothing wrong with it. It is usually a sign that you are doing well. The ego system feels attacked and uses the false guide as a defence. Avoid disappointment, guilt, inadequacy or other stupidities. The ego is a master at spraying such feelings and taking them in would only serve its purpose. And most important: do not fight or argue with the false guide. This is the best way to fall into his trap, as all the false guide wants is to be acknowledged and draw your attention in any possible way. Whenever you meet a false guide, be aware that the Spirit Guide is always very close.

The fact that a Spirit Guide is full of love and acceptance does not mean that he encourages or supports behaviours contrary to your sacred path. His love is toward the essence of your being and true nature, not toward your ego. False guides sometimes tend to inflate the ego with excessive compliments and with roles of superiority. They often express judgements about other people, make comparisons, support magical practices and forecast future events of your life or another's. In brief, false guides discourage any kind of real transformation. The Spirit Guide is always close to you, but is extremely respectful of your privacy. He does not give information or suggestions and does not usually show up, unless you request him to do so. On the contrary, false guides are always ready to tell you what you have to do or how you should be, and can invade your space at any time. Use of verbs such as *have to, should, must* are very common in their language.

According to Edwin Steinbrecher, just as the aspect and the initial personality of the Guide can be identified with the cusp of the ninth house, the characteristics of the false guide seem to correspond to the third house and the natal chart domificated from that point. For example, if the ninth house is in Cancer, the third house is in Capricorn. In this case, and in outline, the Guide may initially appear protective, romantic, nourishing, caring, supportive, whereas the false guide may look austere, inflexible, cold, ambitious, rigid and with a strong sense of discipline.

As an advanced development in the work, if your Guide agrees, it can be helpful to work together with false guides. What counts is that the relationship with the true Guide is strong and that he is always in charge. In this way, instead of fighting, fearing or trying to ignore the false guide, you can take him with you in your journeys. This gives the chance to be aware of where the false guide is, to learn his ways and gradually undo the programmes that were given him in a far distant past and that cause him to behave in the way he does. When you know which parts are at play and where they are, you are in a position of advantage.

The most difficult obstacle in the first stages of work is not that of contacting the Guide or discriminating between him and the false guide. It is managing the power that comes once the connection with the Guide has already taken place. In general, when you achieve your first results, the ego system declares a state of emergency and begins to assail you with a vast repertoire of doubts and rationalisation. This phase often lasts for months and has the function of testing your true motivations. For the majority of people it is very easy to meet the Guide and get significant results. What seems more difficult is to get over the following stage when the mental system goes into panic. In this context the best method is to be constant in the relationship with the Guide, apply with attention and practical common sense the instructions given, acknowledge the results, be confidential about your experiences and avoid any conflict with your rational mind. Far from being an enemy to fight, the rational mind is a precious ally you can use in order to acknowledge that your shamanic experiences are well founded.

Animal Guides

In ancient times, according to the myths of various tribal cultures, men could communicate with animals, plants, minerals, atmospheric events and celestial bodies. Then, as the process of the expansion of separation developed, this connection was cut off. Such a crucial shift seems to be related to the eclipse of nomadism and the advent of agriculture. The societies that developed in those times gradually lost the deep relationship with nature that had characterised their ancestors. Through the metamorphosis produced by trance states it was still possible to occasionally re-establish some form of communication. Then this possibility also became rare, until it was limited to a few shamans. These rare people, by entering into an altered state of conscience, could access that mythic past of communion with all nature and bring wisdom into this separate parallel reality.

In astroshamanism, the Animal Guide may be the Spirit Guide himself or identify an additional role of protection and guidance. Animal Guides are particularly useful in recovering and drawing energy to the physical and emotional plane. To acquire an animal as an ally, and to preserve and strengthen the relationship, constitutes the basis of traditional shamanic work. It represents a primary element of reference and contributes to reinforcing grounding and stability. When this rooting is lacking, those who are open to other dimensions (such as mediums, psychics, channellers) tend to become physically and emotionally unbalanced. In many shamanic traditions the wisdom transmitted by an Animal Guide is considered more important than that of any physical teacher, master or shaman.

Animal Guides usually dwell in the Lower World. They represent the eternal essence of the species to which they belong and not a particular animal. Therefore if I meet a wolf in the Lower World, it is the Wolf and not one among the many possible wolves. Anyone who possesses the power of a wolf, a bear or any other animal can attract the power of the entire species. According to shamanic conventions Animal Guides are wild, untamed animals. Pets or domesticated animals (dogs, cats, chickens, etc.) are not usually included in this category. Also insects, with some exceptions (for instance Spider, Ant, Butterfly), are not regarded as Animal Guides, as they are generally associated with psychic intrusions or grievances.[4]

To call and connect with an Animal Guide various procedures are possible (shamanic journeys, trance dances, vision quests, drumming). What follows is a practice of *animal dance* that employs the Four Directions of the Sacred Circle. It is one among many possibilities and represents a way of calling upon the power of the Animal Guide. It is preferable to practise it at night or in a darkened place lit only by a candle. Face the East holding a rattle in the right hand. Shake the rattle for some minutes, starting from the height of your knees up to that of your head, continuing up and down. The East is associated with Fire and here you find aggressive animals, big predators such as Tiger, Wolf, Lion, Panther, etc. Then move toward the South and call, again shaking the rattle, the animals of the Earth. These animals are usually peaceful and vegetarian (Squirrel, Deer, Marmot, Dormouse, etc.). Then face the West to address fish and animals that live in water (Dolphin, Whale, Seal, etc.), amphibians (Frog, Toad, Newt, Salamander, etc.) and reptiles (Snake, Lizard, Turtle, etc.). To conclude the horizontal axis, face North and call the birds. Then shake the rattle upward (the Higher World), downward (the Lower World) and at the height of your heart (the Middle World). After moving the rattle for some additional minutes, bring your attention to your Intent, stay still and connect with your Function. Then begin to run on the spot for almost five minutes, shaking the rattle and calling the animals of the Four Directions. In the end stop and conclude the ritual. After this practice you can begin to dance your Animal Guide, while shaking a rattle or employing a drumming tape. Dance freely without doing anything special. Once you are involved with the dance it will be possible to perceive, feel or see an animal. The perception can express itself simply with physical feelings or visions. As soon as you enter into this state, invite the animal to have more space in your physical body. The dance lasts a minimum of 15 minutes.

Animal Guides are always beneficial and inoffensive no matter how ferocious they appear. Once you have acquired an Animal Guide, you can travel with an additional support to the inner worlds. To keep the relationship it is advisable to have regular connections with the animal. This means evoking it frequently, drawing and drumming it, singing its chants, expressing its energy in wild places and most of all to dance it, transform into it and let it move through your body. You may even employ your Animal Guide for distant healing work. 'The guardian animal spirit resident in the mind-body of a person wants to have the enjoyment of once again existing in material form. It is a trade-off, for the person gets the power of the whole genius or species of animals represented by that guardian. Just as a human may want to experience non-ordinary reality by becoming a shaman, so too a guardian spirit may wish to experience ordinary reality by entering the body of a living human.'[5]

1 Edwin C. Steinbrecher, *The Inner Guide Meditation: A Spiritual Technology for the 21st Century,* Samuel Weiser, 1988, p. 43.

2 Carl Gustav Jung, *Memories, Dreams, Reflections,* Fontana Press, 1995, pp. 207–208.

3 The Nodes are the points where the Moon's plane of orbit around the Earth intersects the Earth's plane of orbit around the Sun. The Nodes move retrograde, i.e. backward, around the Zodiac and make a complete cycle in 18.6 years. This traditionally provides a time-frame which spans one generation. In the natal chart these two points of intersection always lie in opposition to each other and are called the North Node and South Node. Western astrologers generally interpret the North Node as the future potential, or the direction toward which one is heading, and the South Node as the past, or the direction from which one is coming. Here the South Node is an indicator of old habits, behaviours, or past life patterns which are deeply rooted in the nature of the subject and that need to be balanced or released in the current life. This can occur by developing the qualities corresponding to the position of the North Node. The concept of the Nodes is present in the mythology of all major Indo-European races and finds its oldest documented origin in the Hindu tradition of the *Rig Veda,* although in Hindu astrology the Nodes are given a different interpretation.

In the traditions of the Mexican and Guatemalan Indians a distinction is made between *naguals* and *tonals*. The *nagual* is the term for Animal Guide. *Tonal* (derived from the Aztec *tonalli*) refers to something similar to the Zodiacal sign of birth, which is usually represented by an animal.

4 'The *tonalli* was part of an elaborate calendrical system with implications of predestination, somewhat analogous to one's sign in Western astrology. Thus the tonal concept carries the implications of fate, predestination, and the destiny of one's life from birth to death. [...] Thus one's life experiences in ordinary reality may be believed to be determined by the tonal animal; but this animal is not the same as the nagual of the shaman, which like guardian animal spirits elsewhere is connected with the SSC [shamanic state of consciousness] and, as Castaneda implies, lies beyond ordinary reality.' (Michael Harner, *The Way of the Shaman*, Harper, 1990, p. 63.)

5 Ibid., p. 68.

CHAPTER 7

THE TOTEM SPIRITS

According to astroshamanism, Totem Spirits, or *Paheka* (as they are called in the *Epic of the Sacred Cone*), are the basic archetypes, or gods, and the original models from which all human perceptions and experiences derive. Each one of them is a specific aspect of the Divine as it appears from a limited perspective and portrays a specific emanation of the whole with the function of making it more understandable to our perception which is based on separation. Totem Spirits keep together what our minds consist of, both individual and collective, unconscious or conscious.

Totem Spirits correspond astrologically to planets or constellations and mythologically to the gods of the various civilisations that have developed or arrived on this planet. To the early inhabitants on Earth, they appeared in their pure and visible form. With the reinforcement of the process of separation, these gods assumed frozen representational manifestations or complex patterns that then multiplied abundantly into countless subsidiary types. This process received a major impulse in western culture as a consequence of the expansion of Egyptian, Greek and Roman deities.[1] According to various cosmologies and interpretations of ancient texts or traditions, the awareness of Totem Spirits and basic archetypes was contaminated by alien space travellers who descended on Earth and were then transformed into gods by the religions which developed on this planet. In the epic tales of Mesopotamia, for example, these beings, called the *Anunnaki* ('Those Who from Heaven to Earth

Come'), arrived on Earth about 450,000 years ago to mine gold. According to Zecharia Sitchin, the world-renowned Hebrew scholar and Sumerian translator, these visitors to Earth were not referred as divine beings or 'gods' by the Sumerian culture, and it was mainly through the paganism of Greece and Rome that this identification spread into most human mythologies and belief-systems. Various esoteric sources and interpretations of ancient texts suggest that these alien visitors, often described as reptilian in nature, dismantled the original DNA of humankind and created versions of humans with genetic manipulation. The purpose was to allow them to control the planet, employing humans as slaves, limiting their perception and feeding on their work, bodies, consciousness, fears and emotions.[2] The *Popol Vuh*, the basic text of the Mayan epic, as well as Sumerian and other ancient texts, recounts a similar process in the description of how these 'gods' created mankind to act as slaves for them. The anthropologist Michael Harner, in his early shamanic experience with the Conibo Indians of the Peruvian Amazon, met giant reptilian creatures who explained that 'they were fleeing from something out in space [and] they had come to the planet Earth to escape their enemy. The creatures then showed me how they had created life on the planet in order to hide within the multitudinous forms and thus disguise their presence. [...] I learned that the dragon-like creatures were thus inside of all forms of life, including man. They were the true masters of humanity and the entire planet, they told me. We humans were but the receptacles and servants of these creatures.'[3] Michael Harner was then stunned to find out that the details of his vision were already familiar to the local native shaman whom he contacted to receive a professional opinion.[4]

Since the most ancient times of human history, despite the prevailing distortion of information, the teachings around the basic gods have been transmitted through the work of few individuals or esoteric groups. The number, the form, the name and the function of these original archetypes change according to the traditions to which they belong and their actual strategic role in a context which extends far beyond present human understanding. Even evolved human beings are unable to see Totem Spirits for what they really are and tend to perceive them through the most accessible forms of archetypes in their system of reference (for example, as a Roman or Celtic god, a Major Arcana, a cartoon, a cinema actor, an ET). In most cases Totem Spirits do not meet such acknowledgement and, in order to draw attention to themselves, are then forced to resort to specific people (mother, father, partner, boss, lovers, friends, enemies) or to specific situations (work, education, home, addictions, health problems) found in everyday life. Astroshamanism, as it is described in this introductory text, employs the astrological language as a model of reference and considers twelve basic Totem Spirits to be associated with the twelve zodiacal signs and their ruling planets.

What I perceive as reality now is but a long chain of layers and projections through which the original Totem Spirits reveal themselves. When I give priority to the archetypes, instead of chasing the innumerable mirrors of their projections, life discloses its original essence and my real purpose begins to flourish. In astroshamanism it is vital to explore the sectors and connect with the Totem Spirits only after having established an adequate rapport with the Spirit Guide. There is no danger in such relationships as long as the Guide is present. On the other hand, when I operate on my own and without precautions, the ego can easily manipulate the experience and accidents are likely to occur. The Guide functions as protector, balancer and faithful advisor. His closeness allows the shamanic voyager to operate in conditions of security and supports the release of grievances which block healthy relationships with Totem Spirits. As long as the Guide is actively invited and given permission to work, explorations of sectors are perfectly safe.

To communicate with Totem Spirits it is necessary to develop a sensitivity which requires training and practice. Most of their answers or discourses are expressed through images, sounds, feelings, telepathy and subtle verbal communication. The point here is to acquire the capacity to perceive these messages. The easiest way to understand and integrate them consists in employing all senses, directly connecting with the Guide and following his suggestions. Also it is important to bear in mind that the fundamental nature of these experiences deeply transcends the limitations of perceptions based on duality, or separation.

Relationships with Spirits are not so different from those with human beings. Sometimes it is necessary to be empathic, detached, direct, diplomatic or challenging or to insist, make clear agreements, ask questions, etc. A key in these relationships, as well as in those with physical beings, is love, respect and honour. Totem Spirits, Animal Guides, non-ordinary entities, human friends, and relatives, all respond to the respect that I give them. Most human beings have been taught to prioritise a limited minority of relationships and disregard many others. Over the ages this discrimination has reached such an extent that many living forms are not even seen or considered *real* anymore. I have been influenced for so long by this externally focused world, that it may take some time to mature my true perception and retrieve a full relationship with my Spirit Guide. The channels of communication need to be cleansed, released of ancient debris, healed and reactivated. It is not an instantaneous process and, although some significant results can come about in a short time, the work is to be persisted with for the whole life. However I may see it, the Plan of Salvation has its own way to proceed and this often differs from my limited understanding and perception. Patience, dedication and trust in the Guide are essential ingredients here.

Totem Spirits hold the basic keys of my perception. Their essence is neither good nor evil. Some of them can be sensed in different ways and at times cause major grievances. Here the purpose is to find out why they seem to create troubles and then channel their energy in accordance with a specific Intent connected with the Function. Each Spirit has various qualities and the work is about allowing such qualities to become powerful gifts and medicines available on the spiritual path. Perhaps, I may need to acquire the capacity to detach myself from turbulent emotions and waves of anger that unexpectedly tend to disrupt my life. In this case, for example, the Totem Spirit of Sector 11 (Aquarius) could provide valuable medicines in terms of detachment and ability to face change. The most relevant archetypal energies are usually reflected in the people that I draw to me in my life. For instance, if I spend most of the time writing, meditating, talking or working at a mental level, I may attract friends, people or situations that are very concrete, practical and down to earth. An operative connection with earthy Totem Spirits – like Sector 2 (Taurus), Sector 10 (Capricorn) or Sector 6 (Virgo) – could be favourable here.

The advantage of the work with Totem Spirits is that all the qualities they represent can be sought directly and systematically. The initial purpose of astroshamanism is to lay the foundations for a healing rapport with each archetype. In this preliminary process a good practice consists of acknowledging or naming the Totem Spirits in question and employing the imagination to perceive them as living entities. After all, it was probably our imagination itself which originally gave them form. And it is through the use of this same imagination that I can retrieve the energies of the archetypes and heal what has caused my separation from them. In the first place, I recommend being open to an unbiased experiential relationship with the Totem Spirits, finding out about their nature, getting the gifts they have to offer, releasing possible grievances and spending time discovering more regarding the way they operate in your life. Then, optionally, you can receive additional information through mythological or nature films, articles, books, or by visiting sacred sites, using statues, pictures and other tools related to the archetypes. There is a large amount of material currently available in the market; yet again the precedence is given to your direct relationship with the archetype.

Please keep in mind that what you read throughout this text is mainly the description of a strategy. There are numerous ways to work with archetypes and this is just one of the many possibilities. I remind you to avoid becoming rigid about it. These teachings are by no means an absolute truth. The form of their expression is indeed transitory and provisional. The measure of their value, as with all strategic teachings, is only the degree to which they work for you. In some circumstances it may be more helpful to adapt the practice to your specific situation and process. Also be aware that the work with Totem Spirits can be rather disappointing for people who look for glamour and a sense of grandeur. It is an intense transformational practice that involves facing and releasing deeply rooted emotions and primal experiences. I recommend proceeding with gentleness and, should excessive discomfort ensue, either avoid meeting the Totem Spirit directly and choose other practices (for example, the healing tools provided for each sector in the second book) or operate in close connection with a qualified shamanic operator.

Ancient people offered regular sacrifices to each god or goddess. They knew that neglecting one of them would mean inviting that Spirit to take what was due in an unpredictable and often brutal manner. In such apparently primitive customs lies the understanding of a basic key to the work with Totem Spirits. *Sacrifice* ('to make sacred') here signifies the recognition of a specific energy, accepting relationship with it and acknowledging it as part of me. Robert M. Stein described this process as follows: 'Psychosomatic research has been almost exclusively limited to investigating the mind–body relationship in terms of cause and effect. In contrast to the causal model used in modern scientific medicine, the ancient acausal model of theurgic medicine holds that sickness is a consequence of divine action. A basis of theurgic medicine is that the deity who inflicts the wound is at once both the sickness and the cure. The aim, therefore, is not to combat the disease as in allopathic medicine, but rather to establish a connection, i.e. a *right relationship to the divine power.*'[5] The key here is identifying these psychic energies again, allocating them to their specific realm and choosing to establish a direct relationship. Throughout the ages, sacrificial acts have undergone various developments: from human sacrifices to the offering of animals, plants, stones, food, money, specific abstentions or the release of grievances and of the ego itself. In the end, the Totem Spirits themselves constitute the ultimate sacrificial object.

Figure 4: The Circle of the Totem Spirits

Exploring the Sectors

Voyages to the Twelve Sectors often constitute a natural follow-up of the journey to meet the Guide described in Chapter 6 ('Meeting Your Spirit Guide'). Once the connection with the Guide has been established, the second phase of the work usually consists of exploring the sectors. In practice, this means to have a direct experience of the energy of each sector and to retrieve missing soul parts. This can take place in many ways and is sometimes similar to the traditional shamanic practice of *soul retrieval*. The choice regarding which sector to visit is often determined by the position of the Sun or Moon in the Sky.[6] This means that, unless there are specific needs, or the Guide suggests otherwise, the right time for exploring a sector is generally when the Sun or the Moon is transiting the corresponding sign.

The perception of the characteristics of each sector's territory and the experiences which take place there vary enormously from person to person. According to lineage, ancestors, planetary positions and other data, each individual meets different situations and beings. Various methods of exploration are employed. One initial type involves establishing a connection with the Totem Spirit of each sector. This is generally associated with the traditional astrological ruling planet of the sign: for example, the Moon for Cancer (Sector 4), Saturn for Capricorn (Sector 10). In this instance, it is not necessary to have an individual astrological chart as the Totem Spirits are in the same position for everybody. Another kind of exploration entails meeting the Totem Spirits corresponding to the planets as they are positioned in the natal chart. This means that if I want to meet Saturn, which in my chart is in Sagittarius, I need to go to Sector 9 (i.e. the Sector of Sagittarius), whereas with the previous method I would go to Sector 10 (the ruling Sector of Saturn). A further and more advanced possibility is connecting with two or more Totem Spirits at a time as represented by the position of the Sun and the Moon in the Sky or by planets in aspects. Such meetings are used to heal conflicts among Spirits and concern one of the major features of astroshamanic advanced work: the undoing of the *Paheka Rubhe*.[7]

What follows is merely a model aimed at describing one of the basic practices of initiation to astroshamanism. If you decide to have a complete experiential introduction to this work, you are invited to consider the following essential instructions and use them during your explorations of each sector. Please be aware that you do not need to adhere strictly to this model if you develop or already have one that works better for you. In the beginning what counts is to employ the basic principles. Also you can adapt your practice in accordance with the technique of journeying which you find most effective (lying on the back or face down, sitting or standing, trance dance, chanting, astroshamanic postures, etc.). I invite you to treasure your insights, honouring the validity of your experiences and keeping in mind that in shamanism no one has the authority to challenge them.

Connection with the Totem Spirit

1. Use the sequence of opening for shamanic journeys described in the points from 1 to 7 in Chapter 5 ('Sequence of Opening and Closing for Shamanic Voyages'). If you have your Sacred Circle Pieces, position yourself in front of the piece corresponding to the sector you are exploring. When you connect with your Intent, remember to focus on the purpose of your journey. This could be stated, for example, as follows: 'I intend to visit Sector ... to meet the related Totem Spirit and receive information on my Intent and Function so that I can express my highest potential for the benefit of myself and the whole. I will use the information I get with integrity.'
2. Once you reach the area of the Spirit Circle, go toward the Great Tree at the centre and call upon your Spirit Guide or do what it is your custom to do at this stage.
3. Greet your Guide and establish an energetic connection.
4. Tell your Guide which sector you intend to visit and invite him to accompany you during the journey. Ask if there is something that you need to know before going on. Invite the Guide to offer you protection and direct your way.
5. Follow your Guide as he moves from the Great Tree toward one of the twelve stones of the Spirit Circle. The Guide will point it out in some way. That stone represents the access to the territory of the sector that you have chosen to visit. Look at the stone closely. When you are ready to go, place both your hands on the stone. At this stage the stone is going to move and show the access to a corridor. This corridor leads to a pathway that allows you to reach the territory of the sector.
6. Let the Guide lead you through this pathway. The

characteristics of the way change according to sector and means of transportation. For example, the way can be a narrow corridor, a river, a lake, a road, a railroad, and you can walk, ride, drive, sail, fly.

7. The pathway comes to an end when you reach the territory of the sector. Sometimes you can notice a specific sign that indicates the entrance or border. Whatever you see, always keep the connection with the Guide and, before doing anything, ask for advice.

8. Then you may find a representative of the sector, or *Auxiliary Guide*. He can have the form of an animal, man, woman or whatever. His purpose is that of escorting you within the territory and taking you to the Totem Spirit. As you move with your Spirit Guide and, if you met him, the Auxiliary Guide, be aware of your perceptions: landscape, weather, temperature, colours, animals, plants, sounds, inhabitants and their activities.

9. When you reach the area where the Totem Spirit abides, ask your Guide what to do. For example, you can wait for the Spirit to come and meet you, or you can call him, go directly to see him, offer a sacrifice, pass a test.

10. When you are in front of the Totem Spirit, make sure that your Guide is close to you and, if you do not know what to do, ask him. Generally you are supposed to greet the Totem Spirit and express your Intent. If you feel safe, you can also establish an energetic connection with the Spirit. Then you can communicate with him in the way you prefer. The purpose of the first meeting is that of receiving information on the way in which you can express your highest Intent in the sector concerned and on how you can apply your Function (i.e. releasing the grievances related to that sector). These objectives may develop in accordance with the nature of the three stages of the *Basic Ritual,* described in Chapter 4 ('The Astroshamanic Basic Ritual of the Sacred Cone') and are summed up by three questions that you can ask the Totem Spirit: a) *What is my highest Intent in this sector?* b) *What is my Function and what do I need to release or do to honour my highest Intent here?* c) *What do I need to receive and retrieve from this sector?* The answer may come verbally or in the form of images, sounds, codes, movements, actions, drawings, etc. It can also develop as a soul retrieval journey or as an

experiential access and regression to major events in *past lives* or collective planetary memories. Whatever happens, accept the first answer or sequence that comes to you, even if it seems not to make any sense. Sometimes the way Totem Spirits communicate appears weird or absurd. This is often a strategy to get through the censorship of the ego system. Let go of your usual ways of thinking and be open to the first answer as it develops. If its meaning does not make sense to you, instead of rejecting it or, on the contrary, pretending that you have understood, ask your Guide or the Totem Spirit for further explanation. If you question directly and honestly, you can be sure that you will receive an answer. This generally contains information that identifies your specific potential and the way to develop it. If you are willing to get down to work and practical understanding, it is essential *to ask*. The Guide does not usually provide information if you fail to ask. When you do ask and keep on asking until the answers are clear, you are bound to receive specific suggestions, practices or courses of action. It is good practice to consult your Guide before agreeing to accept whatever the Totem Spirit may invite you to do. If the Spirit corresponds to a planetary energy that is blocked or operates disharmoniously in your system, he could sometimes draw you to do strange and dangerous things, or to act in a way which is contrary to your Intent. In this phase of communication with the Totem Spirit, your aim is to get clear information, which is acceptable both to you and your Guide, about something that you can do practically in your life to express your potential.

11. When you have received the answer, you can invite the Totem Spirit to offer you a gift in the form of a *Spirit Medicine*. It can also be the Spirit himself who gives it to you, or you and your Guide that decide to get it with the consent of the Spirit. It may be a stone, sword, wand, sphere, ring, fruit, plant, etc. It may also be received or retrieved as a fragmented piece of your soul and appear as a younger version of yourself or in the form of an animal or human being. Consider the first object or being that is shown to you and avoid changing it in accordance with your expectations of what you think a Spirit Medicine should be. Before accepting it, ask your Guide if it is appropriate or check within to see whether you feel all right in receiving it. If the answer is negative, thank the Totem Spirit and go to step 12. If the answer is positive, take

the object. The Spirit Medicine is usually an essence which has been adapted to your own nature in order to manifest your potential and release grievances. It allows you to act out the qualities of that sector and to connect with your Intent and Function. When you receive it, examine its shape with care and ask for explanations on its usage or properties. Continue until you have a basic understanding of its functions. Also ask what the name of the Spirit Medicine is. Here you can get a name in your mother tongue or in some other language. Always accept the first name you receive whether it makes sense or not. Often this name is a sort of access code that enables the Spirit Medicine to work. Then you can ask the Totem Spirit to store the Medicine in a place of your body. Be aware of the connection of the Medicine with that specific part of your physical body.

12. In the end, after thanking the Totem Spirit, take leave of him. You can also ask his permission to visit the sector again. He will automatically agree, as this is just a strategic formality that enables you to be clear that you are always welcomed. If you have decided not to accept the Medicine, or your Guide suggested that, you can return at other times and try again.

13. On conclusion of each exploration, it is good practice to ask your Guide if your energies and the exchanges you had with the Spirit are balanced. When you receive something from the inner world it is advisable to know clearly the terms of negotiation and what is to be given as a form of exchange. The Guide will tell you if you remember to ask him. For example, he may invite you to perform a certain action or to offer an object, say a prayer, burn some incense, have a walk in the wood. To receive a Medicine from a Totem Spirit without giving anything in return can appear as an invitation for him to take whatever he wants from you. The range of value for Totem Spirits is quite different than ours: a single hair can be tantamount to a golden ring with diamonds or to a high sum of money. Therefore, to avoid misunderstandings, it is best to be clear as regards the conditions of exchange.

14. Then go back following the same path you used before. If the Auxiliary Guide was with you, take leave when you reach the point where you originally met him. Thank him for his help and then move through the corridor up to the stone of the Spirit Circle. Thank the stone of the sector, place your hands

on it and then close the access. At this stage, if you wish, you can still stay with your Guide for a while and ask questions about your journey. Then come back to your ordinary state of consciousness.

Sector Detectors and Shamanic Forms

I am fed up with your moans! It is extremely tedious to keep hearing stupidities such as 'Your Heinousness, I have been serving in the Provisional Order for ages. How come I am still unable to get rid of projections?' Please, stop this nonsense! Projections are not an epidemic. On this boulder projections are simply a natural phenomena. They are pure oxygen. You cannot do without. Moreover, they constitute one of the chief benefits that attracted you here. Don't you remember? ... Yes, of course, at times your memories are feeble. You beget paraphernalia and then you fail to recall how they function. And you even ask yourself who is that booby that produced those contraptions. Do whatever you want, it is up to you. As for me, my memory is lucid like crystal. I am aware that on Earth I am a spectator of the top hits projections of the galaxy. Not to mention the players: so dramatically involved in their roles, so authentic, flawless. ... Never seen anything like that! You are my favourite comic actors. That's one of the reasons I am taking a break here. I do love to have fun. I've been travelling for ages. Well, indeed, I've never guffawed so much as here on Earth. Your way of acting is superb. You do it in a way that does not look like playing at all. How do you manage it? How is it possible? You are amazing. You are so total. I am fond of you and all your projections. I always find something that shakes me with laughter. Like that chap who, upon waking up to go to work, gets angry with his alarm clock and starts a new world war. Or the other one who, when the weather is fine, falls in love with the barometer and spends nights of passion in its company. Then, when the weather is bad, he gets upset with the barometer and breaks up the relationship due to incompatible sexual attitudes... . (AFS Bogus)[8]

Totem Spirits, or *Paheka,* are the basic archetypes of astroshamanic work. They epically constitute the main horizontal membership who – together with the *Spirit Keepers* (the Four Directions), the mid-points and the vertical membership (the Spirit Guides of the Three Worlds) – are the chief authority in the inner strategic reality represented by the Spirit Circle. This is the operative keyboard of whatever happens in the outer world, or the projector that sends pictures into the screen of ordinary reality. The natures of Totem Spirits are in themselves neutral. Their characteristics change according to the degree of my projections. They may appear as allies or enemies, pleasant or unpleasant, loving or hateful. If my relationship with a Totem Spirit is disturbed, he can manifest in my life with grieving, or *demonic* traits (*Graha*). These aspects are projected on all people or situations that seem to cause fear, repulsion, obsession, hate, dependence, addiction and all kinds of grievance, as they are perceived by the ego. By isolating, hating or repressing these contexts, I fight or suffocate dangerous zones that end up being amplified in my inner world and will eventually find expressions in outside life. Repression becomes like a magnet that draws towards me outer screens upon which I project all my inner, or non-ordinary, undesired contents. Other types of projections, such as those of *special love relationships*, are also the outcome of my interaction with Totem Spirits. Here the positive contents of a Totem Spirit are projected onto a specific human being, situation or aspect of the outer world. What happens is that I see something that exists within or in another dimension through the projection of something that is outside in the ordinary reality. When the projection is pleasant and supportive, this condition causes feelings of well-being and satisfaction. Yet, if I lose sight of the real source of emanation of such a state and limit my awareness to the conventional and outer world, I am bound to experience pain, disruption or misery when the projection changes or comes to an end.

According to astroshamanism the true unfoldment of a spiritual path is not possible as long as I continue to consider the outer visible world as the foundation of my reality. 'As long as unconscious projection is taking place, everyone in your outer world is literally some part of yourself functioning as the perceived ego of the other – *all* are actors in the movie *you* are starring in, taking their positive and negative roles to fit *your* particular movie script. Your current ego (what you presently consider yourself to be) acts as a membrane between the forces flowing out of you onto your world and the forces flowing back onto and into you from the other projecting entities in your personal reality. Until you can experience how your projecting energies are affecting others, you will never understand how their projections are affecting you in turn.'[9]

The subject of projection is one of the basic concepts in astroshamanic work. I have considered it from different perspectives. In the beginning I thought that projection was a psychological disorder which occurred only under certain conditions or with certain people. Then I realised that it was the basic trend in human relationships, although there could always be some exceptions. My experiential understanding now is that there are no exceptions at all and, as far as I can see of life on this planet, projection is not a disorder. On the contrary it is a natural phenomenon for all *body-owners*. What counts is the use I make of, and the awareness I have, of projections. Following this premise, whatever I perceive out in the world, no matter how apparently beautiful or ugly, becomes a screen, or detector, about something which exists within me or on another level of awareness. This creates a web of projections which is indeed the *web of life*. We are all connected by a web which is invisible to ordinary human eyes. Every form that exists, from atom to organism and to the whole universe itself, is connected and determined by a web of invisible units.

I have spent some time experiencing and classifying specific categories of projections. In astroshamanism they are called *detectors* and their function is that of showing me from the outside the state of particular areas in my life as represented by each sector. For example, my mother, my father-in-law, the father of my business-partner, the third brother or sister of my father, or the mother of the mother of my father are all detectors of Sector 4, which is the area related to my roots, past, childhood, home, intimacy and Moon side. Energy detectors have nothing to do with the nature of the persons themselves or the way other people consider or judge them. They are only related to the way I project on them. This scheme of detectors comprises virtually anyone or anything: from my closest relations up to a distant third cousin or even my neighbour's dog and my sister's employer's car. It is a most useful device to bring awareness as regards projections and to help the mind to get acquainted with the web of life and the sectors of the Sacred Circle. All people and situations that move onto the screen of my life – past, present and future – have a specific location in my shamanic inner world. The way in which I perceive them shows me the quality of my relationship with specific Totem Spirits and their related sectors.

In astrology, persons, objects, and all the categories of physical reality that operate as sector detectors can easily be spotted in the natal chart through the system of the *derived houses*.[10] According to this approach, the astrological chart provides all the rough basic information regarding the ordinary as well as the non-ordinary world. All persons, forms or situations as they are met both in dreams, thoughts or in the outer reality, operate as detectors for the corresponding sectors. The detectors related to each sector indicate the state of the particular areas they represent. For example, according to this strategy, if I have a dream where my paternal grandfather (which in this system corresponds to the seventh house) looks very happy or if I meet my maternal grandmother, my wife or former partner (also corresponding to the seventh house) and I perceive any of them as joyful, happy or in a generally good state, it means that similar conditions apply to the areas of life represented by Sector 7 (relationships, marriage, partnerships, contracts, justice, diplomacy, art, kidneys, lower back, etc.). This is a sign that the energies of that sector are *high* and that I can use them or give them away in my horizontal or ordinary life. On the other hand, if I perceive the above subjects in unpleasant situations, this can be an indication that the energy of the sector is *low*. There is nothing wrong about that, as the fact of experiencing *low* and *high* energy is part of the natural laws of balance on this dimension. As long as I do what is needed and do not confuse the detector with the object of its detection, all is very well. It is like when the red light flashes on the car dashboard. It is an indication that I am running out of petrol. It does not mean that there is something wrong with the light. The flashing light provides a most useful service and does an excellent job. Its flashes symbolically represent the reality of a shortage of petrol. They indicate what is going on somewhere else and the action that is to be taken there (i.e. filling the tank in due time, unless I deliberately choose to run out of petrol). It would not make any sense to remove the dashboard and turn the light off. Nor get worried, upset about, or invest all my attention on, the light. Yet this is usually what most human beings do in their lives. They waste enormous quantities of energy dealing with symbols and miss what the symbols are meant to convey. Confusion between symbols and different degrees of reality is the major cause of chaos, frustration and grievances on this planet. The detectors indicate where I need to operate and apply my Function. They symbolically translate the climatic conditions of their sector of reference and give me indications regarding the situation of that area and how I can handle my relationship with its Totem Spirit. When the level of a detector is *low*, it is a sign that I need to connect with my Guide and work directly at the source of the problem. In this case it is often a question of journeying into non-ordinary reality to do what is required: balancing the relationship with a Totem Spirit; facing the equivalent shamanic forms; releasing grievances; connecting with ancestors or other beings; retrieving lost soul parts; etc. Sometimes this would also reflect in taking action in the ordinary reality and doing specific things in the areas of life which have been detected. Whatever I do, it is always essential not to confuse the symbol with what the symbol represents.

The astroshamanic way of helping somebody or of healing a specific situation in the outer reality that is serving as a detector consists of confronting the equivalent *shamanic form*. According to this strategy that form is the representation of one or more Totem Spirits that have probably been neglected or denied. In order to create a connection, that form is forced to manipulate the life or the image of an ordinary person or situation. That person, as I perceive him, is an energetic aspect of myself that is not necessarily related to the real nature of the person concerned. The most widespread and ancient creeds around the origin of illness are unconsciously based on these very premises. For ages it has been believed that sickness occurs as a result of black magic being conducted against somebody. At a shamanic level, although the action of an external enemy can cause considerable harm, the primal cause of the whole process is found and worked at within, through its shamanic form. Whenever I operate with a shamanic form and deal with it in the company of my Guide, I give my contribution for a positive change both in my inner and outer reality. The impact on the outer person, as I work with shamanic forms, is that either I heal my relationship with him or he completely disappears from my life.

During my first months of work as a hotel receptionist, I was strongly disturbed and frustrated by the Assistant Manager. He appeared carping, arrogant and always ready to humiliate the staff with sarcastic remarks and reproaches. I had never perceived in my life such a loathsome person. During the work shifts I felt so annoyed and frustrated. Then, when I was off duty, I would still continue to breed such feelings and infuse them with deep anger and resentment. I repeatedly projected huge amounts of grievances on the screen of my mind and rehearsed scripts of future interactions with the manager. I was obsessed with him. Being my boss at work, he was a detector of Sector 10 (Capricorn) and of its Totem Spirit (Saturn). He operated like the unpleasant sound of a telephone that kept ringing day and night, never leaving me in peace. It took me some time to understand that there was no point in fighting with the phone, and that all I had to do was answer the call. Upon connecting with the Spirit

Guide, I was told that the manager was simply a device activated by Sector 10, i.e. the significator of structure, discipline, commitment, responsibility, authoritative figures, elders, and at a higher level, spiritual masters, Father Sky and even God himself. He reflected the situation of my inner world in that area at that time and the fact that I was disconnected with the energy related with those issues. The manager was simply reminding me of something that I kept disregarding. I asked what that was and my Guide suggested that I meet the shamanic form of the manager. I did so, and was confronted with the image of somebody who immediately reminded me of Marpa, the guru of Milarepa, one of the most popular Tibetan saints. Marpa had a rather severe and tyrannical way of teaching. For example, he would order Milarepa to toil for days in order to build a stone structure, only to have him tear it down again, telling him he had changed his plans and wanted a new structure built somewhere else. The trust of Milarepa was so deep that by surrendering to this outwardly rough master, even in the face of many harsh ordeals, he became enlightened. I was told that what counts is my connection with the inner master. As for the outer authority, it does not matter whether he is enlightened or not. If I have trust, even an unenlightened master can radically transform my life. Sometimes, the fact of being with a true enlightened master can be completely useless. It always depends on me and the relationship with my shamanic world and Guide. I had first heard the Milarepa story some years before at a time when I was desperately looking for a guru. I wanted to be led on a spiritual path and told what to do, but could not find anyone. Upon reading the biography of Milarepa, I made the promise that, if only I could find a guru, I would have followed him even if he were like Marpa. My desire in those days was to go to India to an ashram and serve a spiritual master with total obedience and surrender. Due to some bureaucratic reasons, that would take too long to explain, I could not go to India, at least for some time. I had to stay in my town and release the idea of the master and the ashram. All these problems with the manager were just a projection of my inner frustration. The Guide explained that I had been called to deal with that issue and release the related grievances. He suggested that I manifest my original Intent of serving in an ashram by operating in the shamanic world and surrendering to an inner guru. He advised me to discipline myself and commit to that work. He also explained that the hotel situation was a major opportunity for fulfilling my Intent in the outer reality as well. I could not go to an ashram in India, yet I could change my perception of the hotel and make it an ashram. 'Pretend it is a game. Since you were a child you have always been good at such fictions. And as a matter of fact, it is not a fiction at all.' I followed that advice and started to regularly connect with the shamanic world and employ regular practices. Whenever I felt annoyed with the manager, I would translate his form into that of a hard guru (like Marpa). My imagination was so strong that there were times in which I felt as if the manager was indeed that guru. I could feel a lot of gratitude and compassion for him. Yet I would not give up my dignity, nor act out of fear in my interaction with him as I had done before. I would mainly keep a detached attitude. I regarded my work shifts as a ritual and would operate with total attention, undisturbed by the presence of the manager. But most of all, I would invest a lot of energy in my shamanic world and give priority to the Totem Spirit of Sector 10 and the related shamanic form of the manager. At work I was surprised to witness incredible changes. All the energies that I wasted in clashing with the manager were now directed to my spiritual research. Though I was working as I had always done before, the manager's behaviour towards me totally changed. He began to open himself, developed a strong admiration for me and would even praise me and ask for advice in critical situations. In the end he also shared amazing spiritual secrets with me. I found out that he was indeed a completely different person from what I perceived before. Years later, in another situation, I employed a similar practice with somebody acting as this type of detector. In this case, the person involved was unexpectedly transferred from one department to another. Then after some time he left and I did not see him anymore.

Demons and *Graha*

As an introduction to the topic of this section, I will provide further details about the structure of the *Epic of the Sacred Cone*. These are merely provisional and incomplete fragments of a mythic tradition which it is not my intention to cover in this text. Please be aware that the purpose of the following information is solely strategic and that you do not need to understand or refer to it in order to work with astroshamanism. In the brief cosmological outline of the Epic described in Chapter 2 ('The Vertical Axis and the Three Worlds'), I referred to the *Grey Sphere* as the area of connection between the *White*

Sphere, or *Sphere of Light,* and the *Black Sphere,* or *Sphere of Darkness*. The Grey Sphere is the area where I apparently live as a human being. It is a multi-dimensional reality created by the other two spheres to contribute either to their connection or separation. The structure of the Grey Sphere includes the traditional Three Worlds of the *vertical axis*. The apex of the Higher World is the superior point of the Grey Sphere and corresponds to *Handor,* whereas the apex of the Lower World is the inferior point and is named *Rodnah*. The point at the centre of the Grey Sphere, whose wide circumference at a horizontal level constitutes the Middle World, is called *Pahai*. The Grey Sphere is summarily inhabited by five main typologies of beings: the *Sadoha,* or Spirit Guides (sixth-dimensional entities) consisting of *Ha Sadoha,* white, or light, beings of the Higher World, and *Ma Sadoha,* black, or dark, beings of the Lower World and *Pahai Sadoha,* beings of the Middle World mediating between light and darkness; the *Paheka,* or Totem Spirits (fifth-dimensional entities) divided into the two polarities of *Hare* and *Mare Paheka,* white and black Totem Spirits; the *Graha,* separated fourth-dimensional entities born through the intercourse of the two polarities of Paheka and proliferated into subsequent fragmented three-dimensional variations (like the *Zruddhah,* i.e. humanoids); the *Pahai Etnaire,* multi-dimensional beings and strategic entities purposefully connected with the *Game Resolution* (i.e. the undoing of the illusion of separation and the completion of the *Game of the Sacred Cone*); the *Bhi Jinah,* unifying strategic entities activated by the intercourse of *Pahai Etnaire* and *Sadoha*.

I will focus briefly on *Graha* as in this work their awareness is as crucial as that of the Spirit Guides and Totem Spirits. According to astroshamanism *Graha* can be described as fourth-dimensional entities of apparent antagonism resulting from the projections of our grievances or of what we cannot see when our perception is limited to a three-dimensional level. They feed on our awareness and blur it with the mirage of a separated consciousness. *Graha*[11] is a word that can be translated as 'demons' (from the Greek *daimon*: 'spirit', 'deity') and are experienced as intrusions, emotions, shadows or grievances. They can also be regarded as *waste material* which, once made into *compost,* represent a key substance for creation and growth both at dense and subtle levels. When they are a conscious focus for a luminous Intent connected with the Function, they contribute to the undoing of the painful illusion of separation and the true perception of the loving reality of unity. If this is not the case, they operate as antagonistic forces supporting the hallucination of separation, blocking the portals to the expansion of our consciousness and preventing the connection with Spirit Guides. The transformation of Graha into fertile compost takes place when they are acknowledged as an original creation of ours and released into the *Sacred Cone* (which is a strategic tool aimed at forgiveness and demanifestation of separation). Such operation allows Graha to be directed to those dimensions (like the epic Handor and Rodnah) which can employ them productively in accordance with the Game Resolution. Graha can also be considered as shamanic forms connected with shadow sides of ourselves that do not allow us to access key strategic operative areas so as to avoid causing damage to ourselves and others. Therefore Graha hamper the development of our powers until we find clarity about the purity of our Intent and we are willing to connect it with our Function.

In astroshamanism there are various typologies of Graha. Basically they articulate according to the traditional scheme of *Sadoha* (Spirit Guides) and *Paheka* (Totem Spirits). This means that there are Graha for each sector and world. The Twelve Sectors represent the complete range of awareness in human beings as described by the strategic potential DNA structure of twelve helices. Due to the block, or *Paheka Rubhe,*[12] human beings are limited to a binary helix system. In this polarity of helices, one helix is generally acknowledged as part of the subject's ego identity, whereas the other is projected on the ego identity of another object. The latter identity is part of my awareness, yet I tend to consider it as separated from my identity and cast it upon an object that I perceive as not being me. A significant aspect of the work with the Spirit Guide is that of acknowledging, relating with and integrating this object. In my perception there is no possibility of moving further into the development of human awareness until I decide to uncover and integrate my hidden awareness of the other polarity. In astroshamanic work this split part is called *Mahagraha,* or Grey Demon, and the purpose is to retrieve and transform it into a fully integrated part of my being. When the correspondence of Graha to *Mare Paheka* (black, or negative, polarities) is greater, I call it *Magraha,* or Black Demon, whereas when the correspondence of Graha to *Hare Paheka* (white, or positive, polarities) is greater, I use the term *Hagraha,* or White Demon. Mahagraha (Grey Demon) is therefore a combination which encompasses both Hagraha (White Demon) and Magraha (Black Demon). Establishing a conscious rapport with Mahagraha, in its dual expression of Hagraha and Magraha, releasing the related grievances, and transforming them by tracing back the connection with the Totem Spirits and Spirit Guides of the Lower and Higher Worlds respectively, is astroshamanically as vital as the relationship with the Spirit Guide of the Middle World.

Mahagraha (Grey Demon) appears to gradually take form and develop from the time of birth up to the age of six or seven years. During this time the ego illusion of separation is assimilated and built into the ordinary mind. There, in order to survive, the ego needs a counterbalancing device: that is Mahagraha, which can also be defined as the ego's *double*. Its existence is essential for the ego as it contains all the energies that the ego represses, separates from and refuses to acknowledge as part of itself, no matter whether they are good or bad. It is the primal device of separation and as such is a basic source of embarrassment for the ordinary ego which does its best to keep its nature as unconscious as possible. Each human being lives in constant and close relationship with Mahagraha, although awareness about it is seldom present. Mahagraha expresses itself both in the inner life (through dreams, visions, emotions, thoughts, feelings) and in the outer life. In this latter case it is projected on people with whom I have close relationships (like partners, consorts, lovers, relatives) and on friends, neighbours, strangers met by chance and, due to the influence of mass media, also on celebrities, such as politicians, actors, musicians. The major arena of Mahagraha's projections is generally in the field of partnerships and intimate relationships. There one partner lives out the Mahagraha of the other and vice versa. This process draws a cyclic combination of attraction and repulsion, which is one of the ego's favourite policies for the preservation of its painful existence. When two individuals consciously agree to take back the mutual projections of their Mahagraha and commit to co-operatively work with their Spirit Guides, then we have a *sacred alliance,* or a relationship meant to support the Game Resolution.

According to the system of *sector detectors* and its application as regards partnerships, Mahagraha corresponds mainly to Sector 7 (seventh house). This means that the characteristics of Mahagraha can be broadly described by turning the natal chart upside-down: my Descendant (cusp of the seventh house) becomes its Ascendant, my Midheaven its Immum Coeli, etc. My own astrological chart therefore provides all the rough basic information on my partners, as I perceive them, without the need of studying their own charts. In a woman's chart Mahagraha can also be identified by the position of Mars, whereas in a man's chart it can be associated with the position of Venus.

Here I would like to share some of the early guidance I received on the topic from my Guide.

> *Mahagraha* is a separated and fragmented part that is both projected on your outer and inner environment or inwardly repressed. Mahagraha is humanly perceived as the expression of the energies of various sectors depending on specific factors (such as the cycle of the day, lunar month, solar year). As you allow the energy of Mahagraha to be drawn by the Totem Spirit to whom it refers, you can uncover its ways of operating. When you consciously face Mahagraha you show your willingness to apply your Function. Mahagraha constitutes the basic supplier of energy for the Sacred Cone. By relating with it you become aware of the grievances which have been accumulated and are ready to be released. Please be aware that a grievance is not necessarily something that you perceive as bad. *Graha,* or grievances, are whatever supports the illusion of separation. This means that if you see something beautiful, loving, joyful or ecstatic outside of you and experience yourself as separated from that, well, that is a grievance. Whenever there is the experience of separation, Graha are at work. The ego thrives on separation. Every time you project any part of the Spirit Circle on something outside and separate yourself from it, that is a grievance. The work with Mahagraha consists in allowing all that you have separated from to come back to the original Totem Spirit in the Spirit Circle and then to you. There are two main categories of Graha which can be defined as *Magraha* and *Hagraha*. The former are generally perceived as *bad* or *low*, while the latter are seen as *good* or *high*. Magraha are disposed of through the higher channel of the Sacred Cone leading to Handor, whereas Hagraha are released into the lower channel that descends into Rodnah. [...] A practical way to operate the Sacred Cone and relate with Mahagraha is

that of reviewing both your time of ordinary and non-ordinary awareness. Before going to sleep, after having connected with me, you can call Mahagraha and ask it to show you all the grievances accumulated through the day. Then you gradually review all the people and situations you have separated from during the day. For example, if you met a person and perceived them as being a most loving being, full of wonderful qualities, abundant with joy, etc., and consider that as separated from you, comparing yourself with it, feeling that you are not like it and so on, this is part of the Hagraha. The work to do is to allow the qualities of that person to come back to the basic Totem Spirit and then to you, me, the Earth, the Lower World and Rodnah. If, on the contrary, you see somebody as a hateful person, full of negative qualities or in a state of anger, despair, etc., and regard this as separated from you, judging, making comparisons and so on, that is part of the Magraha. Here again you draw what you perceive in that person to the corresponding Totem Spirit, take it back, give it to me through the Sacred Cone and then to the Sky, the Higher World and Handor. Do this work with me. Do not operate alone, as this can be overwhelming. When we operate daily in this way, Mahagraha is inevitably being cleansed and healed. In the early morning or upon waking up, you can apply the same procedure and work on the content of your dreams. Do this twice a day and whenever it is needed. You do not need to be aware of the detailed technical functioning of this work. What counts is that you give your consent for release to take place. If you firmly state that you are available to let go of all that transits through your system, the work is going to proceed. Another way of carrying this out may be through dance, movements, body postures and intense physical expressions. Connect with me and see what is most appropriate according to circumstances. Regular practices are important as they train you to experience a pattern which will then become spontaneous and part of your life at all times. Releasing is indeed as natural as breathing. Then you acknowledge your involvement with the Game

> Resolution in all moments and acts of your life. [...] Please be aware that the main operational field of the work with Mahagraha is within your Spirit Circle. The world outside gives you the opportunity to monitor Mahagraha. It is a screen where ultimate symbolic manifestations are reproduced. As such it is just the projection of more significant strata that exist somewhere else. Please always remember to be playful and compassionate in the outside world and to do your real work in the inner world. Be a demonstrator outside. If you relate with an outer physical partner, see them as a sacred representation of Mahagraha, and regularly heal your perception. Be joyfully grateful to such partners as they mirror and indicate the operational contents of your Function. The whole illusion of separation is going to demanifest so that the ultimate meeting between Handor and Rodnah can take place. It is a triumphant meeting between two cosmic lovers. And as you heroically move along your path, you become the divine craftsman of this reunion. You dwell in the gap between two cosmic lovers. You are joyfully bound to disappear and melt in the ecstasy of their ultimate encounter. This means that you are truly going to be visible forever and ever.

Facing the Demon

The natural or strategic location of Graha and their negative polarity (Magraha) is identified with the belly area, the emotional realm and the Lower World. This world is traditionally regarded as the place of the instinctive knowledge of the Earth, our animal powers, the inner child, our ancestors and the ancient inhabitants of this planet. In the western culture the Lower World has been severed from ordinary awareness. A significant part of astroshamanic work entails retrieving the relationship with this forgotten dimension and releasing its demonic aspect (Magraha). In this context the work consists of transforming Magraha with a precious figure of support: the Spirit Guide of the Lower World. The meeting with this Guide requires becoming aware of what has been hidden or denied both in our individual awareness and in the collective consciousness of this planet. Once the exploration of the sectors and a relationship with each Totem Spirit has taken place, astroshamanic work involves dealing with the Lower World and its secrets. This is generally a topic for more advanced work and what I define as the Second Level of astroshamanism.

A conscious rapport with Mahagraha is the key for effectively releasing grievances and achieving happiness in all kinds of relationship. Connecting with Mahagraha is a more vertical development of the relationship with Totem Spirits, shamanic forms and sector detectors. What follows is a model that you can employ as reference in the rapport with Mahagraha.

1. Use the sequence of opening for shamanic journeys described in the points from 1 to 7 in Chapter 5 ('Sequence of Opening and Closing for Shamanic Voyages') or employ whatever works for you. If you have your Sacred Circle Pieces, position yourself in front of the piece corresponding to the sector that you are currently exploring. When you connect with your Intent, remember to focus on the purpose of your journey. In this case it can be stated as follows: 'I intend to connect with my Spirit Guide to meet Mahagraha, receive information on how I can heal this relationship and operate in accordance with my Intent and Function.'

2. Once you reach the area of the Spirit Circle, go toward the Great Tree at the centre and call upon your Guide or do what it is your custom to do at this stage.

3. Greet your Guide and establish an energetic connection.

4. Request your Guide to summon your Mahagraha. Ask your Guide if there is something that you need to know before you meet Mahagraha. Invite your Guide to offer you protection and direct your way.

5. When you are in front of Mahagraha, make sure that your Guide is close to you and, if you do not know what to do, ask him. Generally you are supposed to greet Mahagraha and express your Intent. Find the way that best suits you. The purpose of the first meeting is usually that of asking Mahagraha what conditions are required in order to create a mutually harmonious relationship. Accept the answers that you receive, even if they seem not to make much sense. If this is the case, instead of rejecting what happens or, on the contrary, gullibly accepting it, ask your Spirit Guide or Mahagraha for further explanation. If you question directly, you can be sure that you will receive an answer. The same attitude employed in relating with Totem Spirits applies here

as well. Always remember to consult your Spirit Guide before agreeing to accept whatever Mahagraha may invite you to do. You can also make an accord together: for example, deciding to meet regularly or to take a walk in nature every other day.

6. At the end, ask your Spirit Guide to balance the energies that you share with Mahagraha. For example, you can take Mahagraha's hand in your left hand, and the Spirit Guide's in your right, spending some time in silence or chanting.
7. Then conclude the experience according to your usual way of closing and come back to your ordinary state of consciousness.

The first time I met Mahagraha, he appeared to me as a slim, badly dressed man, wearing a black hat. I invited him to sit with me at a table. He then took off his hat, put it on the table and began to extract, one by one, all the grievances of the day. I bought a similar hat while I was visiting Athens. I wanted something waterproof to put on my head so as to be well equipped to face the Scottish weather. That hat was indeed a reminder of the vital need to deepen the connection with Mahagraha. As a matter of fact the person who inspired the purchase of that hat was a major reflection of Mahagraha. Then a series of events brought me to release the hat as well as that person.

White Demons

As we have seen in the previous paragraphs, Hagraha, or the *White Demon*, is one of the two categories of Graha, or grievances (the other being Magraha, or *Black Demon*). Magraha relate to what is usually perceived as negative, whereas Hagraha represent the positive side. For example, if I perceive my partners as beautiful, loving, wise, devoted and compassionate beings, full of luminous talents and abundant with joy, that is certainly great! Yet, if I consider their qualities as separated from me, feeling that I am not as good as they are, making comparisons, projecting all the beauty of the universe on them, and cutting myself off from experiencing those qualities as part of me, well that is Hagraha. The natural location of Hagraha is often identified with the head area, the mental realm and the Higher World. Whereas in the Lower World I deal primarily with emotional waste material and Magraha, in the Higher World I am often confronted with mental residues and Hagraha. So what can I do when this happens? This is very subtle and often risks going unnoticed; yet it represents one of the major aspects of shamanic work. Whenever I see something positive in other people, one thing is 100% sure: they are reflecting back parts of myself. They operate as mirrors and allow me to know something about me. This means that, in order to honour them and myself, I need to retrieve and own the qualities that they reflect. A good practice is that of connecting with the shamanic forms to which they correspond in your Spirit Circle and allowing them to be consciously acknowledged. Another option is that of imitating these beautiful people and using some of their expressions, gestures or ways of doing things. As in the case of Magraha, the work consists of transforming Hagraha with another precious figure of support: the Spirit Guide of the Higher World. The meeting with this Guide involves gradually becoming aware of my ancient origins and of powers which abundantly exceed my current perception. This also tends to be a matter for more advanced work and what I define as the Second Level of astroshamanism.

1 The astrology that has come down to us is mainly the product of Greek writers and philosophers of whose myths and world-views it reflects. The astrological planets themselves are named after the deities of Rome, who were borrowed from the Greek pantheon after the downfall of that culture. Astrology finds its roots in much more ancient times, but its original knowledge was lost. Only a few fragments of that heritage were preserved and adapted to the belief systems based on separation of the following ages.

2 See, for example, Zecharia Sitchin, *The Twelfth Planet*, Avon Books, 1976; Arthur David Horn, *Humanity's Extraterrestrial Origins: ET Influences on Humankind's Biological and Cultural Evolution,* Silberschnur, 1994; William Bramley, *The Gods of Eden,* Avon Books, 1989.

3 Michael Harner, *The Way of the Shaman*, Harper, 1990, pp. 4–5.

4 Regarding the giant reptilian creatures that boasted that they were the true masters of humanity, the local shaman said 'Oh, they're always saying that. But they are only the Masters of Outer Darkness'. (Ibid. p. 7)

5 Robert M. Stein, 'Body and Psyche: An Archetypal View of Psychosomatic Phenomena' in *Spring,* 1976, quoted in Stephen Arroyo, *Astrology, Karma, and Transformation: the Inner Dimensions of the Birth-Chart,* CRCS, 1992, p. 25.

6 To find out the exact position of these two celestial bodies you can employ an astrological calendar or the astronomical ephemeris.

7 See Chapter 2, note 7.

8 Translation and adaptation from Rev. Francesko Saint (ed.), *The Provisional Teachings of His Heinousness the Supply Vicar AFS Bogus,* discourse no. 7, year 1984, in *ProvOrdo Etnai Pratinindhe Pradhikara's Southern Europe Archives for the Year 1984*, Anaghaseva, 1985.

9 Edwin C. Steinbrecher, *The Inner Guide Meditation: A Spiritual Technology for the 21st Century,* Samuel Weiser, 1988, pp. 19–21.

10 The technique of *derived houses* consists of examining each of the 12 astrological houses as the Ascendant of a further cycle of 12 houses, making a total of 144 houses. This traditional method was introduced by Eudes Picard (see: Eudes Picard, *Astrologie Judiciare*, Leymarié, Paris, 1936). It has also been used by Edwin C. Steinbrecher (see Steinbrecher, *Inner Guide Meditation*), though with some differences in the allocation of houses. A list of the sector detectors for each sector is given in Book Two.

11 *Grah* and *graha* in Sanskrit mean 'to grasp' and 'that who grasps' respectively. In traditional Hinduism this word is employed to describe various demons, or malefic spirits, that enter inside their victims causing pain and misfortune. These demons were then associated with the constellations of Indian astrology.

12 See Chapter 2, note 7.

CHAPTER 8

SPIRIT MEDICINES AND SACRED TOOLS

Spirit Medicines

In astroshamanism one of the major phases in the voyage into a sector is when, after having connected with a Totem Spirit (*Paheka*), I ask him for, or get, a *Spirit Medicine,* or *Pahai Tulah*. Spirit Medicines can appear in a large variety of forms: for example as swords, rings, plants, flowers, wands, spheres, keys, books, animals, beings. They are connected with the development of potentials and blessings related to a specific Totem Spirit. Before accepting a Spirit Medicine, I check within or ask my Spirit Guide if it is right to receive it. If this is the case, then I ask the Totem Spirit how to use the medicine, what is its purpose and its effects and what is its name. It is important that I get clear about the Medicine. This does not mean that I have to understand everything. Often the replies from Totem Spirits appear rather enigmatic at first. This is due to the fact that communication with other realms is contaminated and distorted by the ego's thought system. To reach me the Totem Spirit has to employ a code or metaphor. When I open myself and leap beyond the thick layers of the conditioned mind, answers arrive with clarity. Sometimes this does not occur and that is also right.

Understanding requires time and more will become clear at a later stage. Usually the true nature of a Spirit Medicine reveals itself through practice and experience. After I have received sufficient explanation and insight from the Totem Spirit, I ask him to insert the Spirit Medicine into a part of my body. This is indeed a very ancient shamanic practice which can develop in different ways.

The Spirit Medicines placed in the left side of the body tend to relate with instinctive abilities and powers. They function automatically and without any conscious effort on my part. This means that they can be employed spontaneously and without a deliberate decision. Often it is as if they are controlled or manipulated by unknown forces. The Spirit Medicines on the left side seem to relate to the Lower World polarity of the Totem Spirit (*Mare Paheka*), who is often symbolically represented with a female vehicle. Such medicines may be stimulated, enhanced, blocked or affected by relationships with women or beings with a female nature. I have often received the physical representation of some medicines as presents from women (who did not consciously know anything about the nature of my medicine). Astrologically these medicines are associated with the Moon, the planets and signs on the Ascendant, Immum Coeli, South Node and with the non-ordinary traits described in Chapter 10.

The Spirit Medicines placed in the right side of the body seem to require a conscious decision or a training process to work. They relate to Totem Spirits of the Higher World polarity (*Hare Paheka*), who tend to be symbolically represented with a male vehicle. Such medicines can often be supported or blocked by men or beings with a male nature. They are associated with the Sun, the North Node, planets and signs on the Medium Coeli or Descendant.

When Spirit Medicines are inserted in a central position, they tend to relate to both types of Totem Spirits and operate with more balance. Through practice and experience, the position of medicines is likely to extend toward the centre and the opposite side of the body.

The essential astroshamanic initiatory work at the First Level consists of visiting the Twelve Sectors and getting, whenever possible, a Spirit Medicine from each Totem Spirit. I suggest using the medicines regularly and taking note of what happens in your journal. Usually, after a first experimental stage, medicines begin to work effectively and produce considerable healing experiences. If this does not happen, it is necessary to connect with the Guide and the Spirit Totem to find out why. It is preferable not to be passive when there are apparent failures or problems. The best way is generally that of asking directly those who can provide an answer. This means going to the Totem Spirit who gave you the medicine and calling for explanations.

Sacred Tools

Spirit Medicines have shamanic, or inner, forms which also correspond to outer forms. The first outer form that they assume is related to their specific position of activation in the physical body. That point is defined here as a *Sacred Implanted Tool,* i.e. a physical manifestation of a Spirit Medicine.[1] In this context the physical body potentially incorporates in itself all Spirit Medicines and Sacred Tools. Before getting involved with other external tools, the major strategic priority in this context is to be aware of the tools as they exist at a non-physical, or shamanic level (Spirit Medicines) and of the implants as they are represented in parts of the body. Hands, feet, legs, head, belly and so on are much more significant than any other possible Sacred Tool. According to this strategy, only when I use my body as a collection of parts to express my Intent and Function, can I extend it effectively to tools that exist in the physical reality. In this tradition it is not advisable to accumulate too many Sacred Tools, unless you find that this really nourishes and supports you. 'My body is enough,' says Ur Kraab. 'Bones–crystals, breath–incense, heart–drum, hand–rattle, leg–wands, skin–medicine shield and many other items; each being receives from the Paheka all the tools he needs. This body is the altar and the shamanic bag which features them all. Do not look for them elsewhere. Stay within the radius of your land and learn to acknowledge its tools. Allow their power to circulate and share it with others.'[2]

To summarise, I receive power from a Totem Spirit in the strategic form of a Spirit Medicine that exists in the shamanic reality and that reflects itself in the different layers of my body until it reaches the physical one and takes the form of a Sacred Implanted Tool. The latter can transfer the power it represents onto other objects, i.e. *Sacred Tools,* or *Pahai Rupah,* that will then reverse the process and pass it on to subtler levels until it reaches the Totem Spirit again and so on in a spiral process.

Spirit Medicines and Sacred Tools are all used to catalyse and allow the energy to flow. Their function is not that of possessing power. They operate so that power can circulate and be employed for an Intent connected with the Function. In astroshamanic work power is not measured according to its capacity to be kept or accumulated. The strength of Sacred Tools depends on their capacity to work as focused channels. They are strategic representations of the Intent and Function. Each time I see, touch, hear or feel them, they remind me of my connection with the Guide, the Totem Spirit involved and my Intent and Function. They allow me to remember my highest agreements and visions. They also broadcast all that they represent and draw related conditions in my life.

A Sacred Tool can be any material object that is activated for such a purpose (a crystal, drum, stone, wand, rattle, ring, etc.). The most powerful (Sacred Implanted Tools) are found in the physical body and correspond to parts that can be used for shamanic and healing purposes, for example: a hand to give a healing massage, the voice to send out sacred chanting and words, the legs to dance. In times of political, social or religious persecutions and in situations of conflict among sorcerers, in order to protect, or divert the attention from, such precious tools, it became a safety measure to produce and employ auxiliary tools such as: drums, rattles, knives, wands, spheres, rosaries, arrows, candles, temples and sacred buildings. Please be aware that according to a wider perspective, the physical body is also an auxiliary tool.

Sacred Tools are often kept in special containers, or *medicine bags*. The bag itself may represent a Sacred Tool and it is ideal to choose it with this awareness. The characteristic of Sacred Tools is that they are only employed for shamanic or healing work and never to display power or to make a good impression on others. It is also advisable not to talk about them, to keep them with care and spend time in their company. At the same time it is of paramount importance not to get conditioned by them. They are merely toys for playing a game. For this purpose certain Sacred Tools are used and specific agreements are needed which the players concur with when they allow games to be games. There are many games. When I play one of them, it is my responsibility and out of sheer choice. This allows me to be totally present and honour the game together with all its participants. This also means that I need to be aware that it is always me that decides to play the game and not the other way around.

In the following pages I provide a brief description of some Sacred Tools which are often employed in astroshamanic work.

In astroshamanism, after the physical body itself, the Sacred Circle Pieces (see Chapter 4, 'The Sacred Circle Pieces') represent the basic tools. These pieces can also further expand into a collection of Sacred Tools. Together with the pieces representing the sectors, it is possible to assemble tools connected with Spirit Medicines and body parts.

Altars

The altar represents the most prominent and dominant spot in a temple or church. At a vertical level it corresponds to the central point of the spiral, or Sacred Cone. Through that centre, related to the heart, all possible manifestations of energy are focused and directed. It is a catalyser of sacred forces and reproduces the essence of the structure of the Sacred Circle itself. In ritual practices, the altar constitutes the focal point of mediation between Heaven and Earth, the dominant position which enables the exchange between dimensions. It can be likened to a dining table where Totem Spirits and unseen beings consume the offerings bestowed by humankind and then leave their gifts in exchange. The building and arrangement of the altar is often the basis for the creation of sacred spaces. As with all tools of power, its characteristics vary according to each tradition, the nature of the owner or environment, and the specific operative needs. The altar of my sanctuary in Bologna, for example, is a big chest of drawers that belonged to Nonna Iole, my maternal grandmother. It has four large drawers (one for each element) and a massive, simple and rustic shape, which conveys an immediate sense of grounding. Tables, stones, planks, shelves, boxes, stools, carpets, logs, and whatever is truly inspiring for you can be used as an altar.

In many temples and cathedrals the main altar is often located in the eastern area as a way to designate the rising Sun and the direction of Heaven. In astroshamanic work, when I do employ an altar, I tend to locate it in the East, the North or in the middle of the Sacred Circle. More elaborate arrangements include one altar for each direction, whereas at a simpler level the area within the Sacred Circle itself is used as an altar. Many traditions require the altar to be located in a ceremonial zone where only priests or a few chosen people are admitted. Altars are very powerful strategic tools and in order to permit an effective functioning of ritual practices, it is essential to treat them with respect and care. This does not mean that the power of an altar derives from its formal or physical aspect. What counts is always my Intent in activating or using it. If I live with other people or in a limited space, I can simply employ, for example, a portion of my bedside table for this purpose. There I can lay a small silk handkerchief with some significant objects (a stone, a statue, etc.) or, if I want it to be more discreet, I can use a drawer as an altar and open it only during my rituals. It is important not to get fanatical about altars or any other ritual implement. Their purpose is to make things easier and sacred, and not to create complications and grievances. Please also be aware that to do astroshamanic work it is not at all mandatory to have an altar. Use it only if it appeals to you or if your Spirit Guide invites you to do so.

The altar is often employed in astroshamanic work as a way to keep and honour your Sacred Tools and all objects aimed at supporting the relationship with the Spirit Guide and Circle. Some of these objects represent the Four Elements, the Three Worlds, the Twelve Sectors and the medicines of Totem Spirits. For the elements some examples of suitable objects are: candles, lamps, boxes of matches, pieces of flint (Fire); fans, feathers, bells, books or some incense (Air); salt, dishes, stones, grains, crystals, pots with sand (Earth); chalices, shells, cups, essential oils, glasses of water (Water). Statues, gems, rattles, rosaries, etc., can also generally be used. Besides keeping some permanent objects on the altar, I can employ others in accordance with the seasonal rhythms of the year. Each month or season could be the occasion for changing or renewing the altar by using suitable seasonal objects, for example the items related to the correspondences of animals, stones, spirits, plants, listed in Book Two.

In my first years of work with astroshamanism, I used to fix a special panel to the wall above the altar. There I had drawn a zodiacal circle with specific markers (one for each planet) that I would shift according to the motion of the planets. It was a complex galactic watch composed of 16 hands (the 10 major astrological planets plus the five asteroids and the North Node). Then, for the same purpose, I began to employ a ravishing piece of embroidery, made on purpose by Rosaria, Grazia Romano's mother, and depicting all the signs of the Zodiac. Around that I arranged and moved the planets represented by 16 coloured stones. I employed that circle also to activate sacred objects or to provide healing to people or situations identified with specific markers. I still have that embroidery and I use it often as a Sacred Circle in my workshops. It is important for me to take care of these objects, but not to regard them as my property. I am only their custodian and, as such, I need to be aware that at any time I could be asked to release them. A few months after my arrival in Findhorn, I lost this embroidery. I looked for it everywhere and also posted a notice on the community board, but neither I nor anyone else could find it. I received guidance to wait until the eve of the day of my next workshop and, if the embroidery did not show up, to release it and find a suitable substitute. When that day came, there was still no trace of my precious tool. For me it was a sign that I had to release it. I was sad, for I associated that embroidery with many pleasant memories. I also felt its loss could perhaps indicate that I had to stop working with astroshamanism. This generated some confusion in me. Upon asking for guidance, I was told that the embroidery was below the earth as it needed purification. I was to dedicate it to the Earth as a memorial to my surrender to Spirit. Finally, I resigned myself to seeking an alternative tool. I decided to collect some stones for the purpose. As I was collecting them, I heard a voice whispering 'Why are you picking up these stones? The eve is not over yet!' 'When is the eve over then?' I asked. The reply was: 'The eve is over the moment you return to your room tonight.' Then I went home through the woods to my room in Drumduan House. Upon entering the corridor, I saw something in front of the door. With my heart beating at high speed, I moved closer. There I found the embroidery together with the yellow folder I used to keep it in. The folder was almost disintegrated by water and mud, whereas the embroidery was just a bit dirty. Abundant tears poured from my eyes. The identity of the person who found my Sacred Tool remained unknown to me for more than a year until, as I was talking about this episode during a workshop, one of the participants admitted that she was the one who found it.

Power Points

Altars or Sacred Circles can also be built in nature places and power points. In this case they can become a magnet for healing and transformational energies. Nature altars are generally simple and not invasive of the environment. As they work as conduits for exchanges of energies, they usually incorporate a structure that comprises the horizontal as well as the vertical axis. Natural objects representing the vertical plane can be found directly on the spot, for example, the trunk of a tree, a big stone, or a pointed rock. If such a natural axis is not available, it can be set up by erecting a pole or placing a standing stone.

If I am arranging an altar or a Sacred Circle in nature, I prefer to go to a place where I am not likely to meet too many people. I sit or stand there and do some form of cleansing. I close my eyes and connect with my Spirit Guide and Spirit Circle, extending that connection to the environment and the Earth around me. After having asked to be guided to the nearest place of power, I open my eyes and allow myself to be led there. I can have an image of where that spot is, be drawn to move in a specific direction or get a sudden flash as I walk. Whatever occurs, I trust my intuition. When I find the point of power, I usually stand or sit down, connect with my Spirit Circle and align it with the outer environment. If I sense that I need to move a bit farther, I do so. The connection with the Spirit Circle always needs to prevail. I do my best not to be decoyed by the outer appearance of the place and allow my inner relationship to establish exactly where the power point is.[3] Once I get it, I ask the Earth for permission to use the area in accordance to my Intent connected with the Function. I wait for an answer in my heart. If the answer is positive, I give something in exchange. Specific items can be used for this purpose, like seeds, stones or other natural objects. For example, I often carry a small bag of spelt-wheat seeds and give away 3, 7 or 13 according to circumstances. I can also give my saliva or a hair. Permission to use an area is usually given, as nature seems to be delighted when it is acknowledged as sacred space. How do I receive permission or indication that a place is right? It can be through a feeling of easiness, acceptance or well-being, or I can perceive my Spirit Guide nodding or an affirmative whisper from the Earth. There is not a specific model, and what I generally do is to trust my intuition without questioning it with too many thoughts. This is a lesson I have learned through experience and, here, I would like to share one example.

Years ago I received guidance to set, dedicate and honour 13 power points (representing the Twelve Sectors and the Centre) around Parco Talon, a large park at the periphery of Bologna in Italy. These power points comprised a tree and an adjacent altar that I would set up very simply with a few stones, twigs, etc. I first began with the central power point. Then every month, for one year, I would find and activate another power point on the entrance of the Sun into a new zodiacal sign. During my search for the power point of Sector 3 (Gemini), I walked into an area of the park which was totally unfamiliar to me. I chose a path which gradually uncovered an amazing view of the valley of the river Reno. I felt so excited and looked forward to finding a place with the best possible view. As I was starting to hike uphill, my attention was suddenly attracted by a very narrow path leading toward a hillock. I received a simple and clear inner signal that I was to stop and move in that direction, as that was the place I was looking for. Yet, I felt disappointed, for that hillock was cut off from the glamorous sights that were developing ahead. I could not accept that. 'It is too early. That makes it too easy. I have just begun my search and there are such beautiful sights and places ahead. It is probably a decoy and surely I am going to find a better place if only I walk a bit farther?' Therefore, I decided to continue along the main path. The landscape was superb and I enjoyed it for a while. Then things changed. I began to feel frustrated as, after walking for more than three hours, I had not found anything suitable as a power point. Moreover all kinds of misadventures happened. I was trapped in a blackberry bush and scratched myself; I lost my journal and spent one hour looking for it; I was beguiled into taking different paths which, after some initial excitement, revealed themselves to be totally unsuitable. In the end I was worn out, depressed, angry and confused. It was very hot, I was thirsty and didn't have any water with me. Out of sheer exhaustion my mind went blank. I then recollected the images of a television movie that I saw when I was a child. It was about Ulysses and his adventures. I remembered a scene in which he was totally exhausted in a boat in the middle of the sea. In that dramatic moment he had a sudden glimpse of his wife Penelope waiting for him in Ithaca. Out of that glimpse, he managed to retrieve his forces and move forward again. After those sequences, I had a flash of that narrow path which I had seen at the start of my search. At once I heard a magpie singing very loudly. It sounded like: 'That is the place of the power point!' I had lost my bearings and I did not remember where the place was. All I knew is that I had to find it at all costs. I brought my attention to my belly area to raise energy and then began to march like a dauntless warrior. I called upon the spirit of Ulysses to be with me and kept chanting his name together with some potent words in sacred idiom. After a long hike, I retraced my steps to the narrow path. I approached the hillock with a sense of deep solemnity. At the top, I found a very simple, yet proud tree. On one of its branches there was a worn out purple ribbon that somebody had probably placed there a long time ago. 'This is indeed the power point!' I cried out. I then moved around the tree. On the other side I was surprised to find some letters deeply cut in the bark of the trunk. At first sight I was disturbed, for I considered it a lack of respect to do such things to trees. Then, upon reading the letters, I began to pinch myself to check whether I was in a trance state or not. The letters were *U, L, I, S, S, E*, that is *Ulisse*.[4] I stretched my trembling hand out to touch the bark and when I realised that the letters were really there, my body began to shiver and I felt faint. Rotten thought forms in my mind disintegrated themselves at that sight, as my heart opened to receive their remnants. Ecstatic moments beyond any attempt of description followed. That tree is still there. Its blissful teaching is carved in the trunk.

On a much smaller scale, a search can be done also when choosing the location of the power point for the altar in your home. As with a place in nature, I identify the area of my home that has most power as a result of my connection with the Spirit Circle. If I spot a place which is appropriate or practical, I locate my altar there. If the power point is not ideal for arranging an altar, I use it to centre myself, to draw or release energy, and as a bridge between my Spirit Circle and the outside reality. As for the altar, in this case, I set it in a more convenient place and plug it in energetically to the power point. It is like a piece of electronic equipment. If I want to set up a computer (altar) in the house, either I connect it right to the place where the socket (power point) is or, if the socket is in a position where it is not convenient to site the computer, I use an extension and move the computer to a more suitable place. I find that this is often the case for many sacred spaces and I see it as a strategy to prevent abuses. What is apparently prominent (a huge temple, an impressive circle of stones, a majestic pyramid, etc.) may not necessarily correspond to a power point. Often, it can be just a peripheral device or projection screen, whose true source of power is located in an area devoid of any glamour and apparently insignificant. The periphery has a formal, practical or symbolic role, or operates as decoy for those who do not have spiritual sight. In this way, the destruction or misuse of a sacred site does not affect the original power point, of which only a small minority are aware.

The Shamanic Drum and Rattle

The drum represents the most ancient form of human musical expression and is one of the major tools employed by shamans and healers of all cultures. Whereas the rattle is generally associated with the high-frequency energy of the Sky, or Higher World, the drum is usually related to the low-frequency energy of the Earth, or Lower World. It is believed that the drum draws in Earth energies and the rattle attracts Sky, or Higher energies. Drum beats are reminiscent of those of our heart and the inner core of this planet. The dream also creates the acoustic environment of our prenatal stage and the first sound we heard: the beat of our mother's heart. As it is often the most important instrument of a shaman, the drum is regarded with extreme respect. It is frequently identified as a means of transportation (a horse, deer, for instance) that allows the passage along the vertical axis, or Great Tree, and the connection between Sky and Earth. As the bone structure of the drum comes from the wood of a tree, when the shaman beats his drum he is projected into the dimension of the Great Tree. There he can descend, ascend and move in the whole cosmology of the spheres. According to shamanic cosmology there are three basic areas, the Three Worlds (Higher, Middle and Lower Worlds) linked together by a vertical axis which is commonly referred to as the Tree of the World, or Great Tree. In the *Epic of the Sacred Cone*, this represents the umbilical cord of the illusive universe born out of the separation. The purpose is to move back through this channel and release the different stages of the separation so as to finally return to the full awareness of unity. It is the journey to the original land or home. Through the sound of the drum, the shaman moves up and down the Great Tree, communicating with the various worlds, connecting the fragmented parts of the puzzle, restoring the reality of unity and undoing all that has been manifested since separation started. The drum constitutes a microcosm of the multi-dimensional universe whose entire cosmology is represented in the drum itself. In a two-headed drum, one side may produce a higher, positive, yang tone that is connected to the Higher World, whereas the opposite side may send out a deeper, negative, yin tone related to the Lower World. The rim of the drum can be related to the horizontal axis, the Middle World, the surface of the Earth and the trunk of the Great Tree. It operates as the linking agent between higher and lower realms, restoring the balance of polarities and annihilating their illusive separation. The Higher World side of the drum facilitates the capacity of vision and the opening of the higher centres, or the higher chakras, whereas the Lower World side tends to develop primal energy in the lower chakras which can then be directed to the higher centres. The two-headed drum produces deep tones and is widely used for shamanic purposes. The single-headed drum, besides being a traditional instrument used by Irish and Scottish musicians, is prevalent among Eskimo and Siberian shamans, and among shamans from Native American peoples such as the Lakota, Blackfeet and Northwest or Alaskan tribes. Here the upper half of the drumhead usually represents the Higher World, while the lower half identifies the Lower World. These two sides are often painted differently or have indicators that allow the shaman to understand which is which. Also be aware that categorisations and physical identifications in shamanic drums are not at all rigid, as it is always the Intent of the shaman that shapes the reality. Therefore, no matter on which side, or half, of the drum I beat, if I focus my consciousness on the Higher World, that is the area that is going to be activated.

There are different types of shamanic drums. Traditional drums are circular or oval, and are held in the left hand, leaving the other hand free to beat the drum, generally with a stick that some shamans call a *whip*. Two basic models are available for purchase: rawhide drums and synthetic drums. The latter are inexpensive, single-headed drums with a mylar head and are easy to beat, especially for beginners. Rawhide drums produce a much more articulate and powerful sound, yet they do not have a fixed pitch and are very sensitive to variations in temperature or weather conditions. Their energy varies according to the type of leather or wood: goat, deer, horse and shark have different energies, as do oak and maple. Although diverse in terms of energy, both rawhide and synthetic drums are equally effective for shamanic work.

Different types of sounds are produced according to the area of the drum which is played and the inclination of the drumstick. Usually, the central part generates a deep sound, whereas as you proceed closer to the edge, the tone becomes more and more acute or bell-like. I prefer to hold the stick gently and allow gravity to prevail rather than imposing my control. The sound of the drum can generate frequencies in the theta wave range (four to seven cycles per second) which induce a deep trance state or perception of non-ordinary realities, as well as in the alpha wave range (seven to thirteen cycle per second). The latter is the primary frequency engendered by Earth's electromagnetic field and generally produces light trance and ideal conditions for shamanic experiences.[5] This feature makes the drum a precious companion in shamanic journeys, healing work and rituals. Some shamans also employ it for divinatory purposes. For example, they toss the drumstick and take decisions according to the position it lands.

Before starting to beat the drum, unless it has a synthetic head, check if the drum is flat. If this is the case, you can dry it out by gently exposing it to a source of heat (a candle, fireplace, etc.), putting your hand in between to test the temperature. If the drum is too dry, you can spray it with water and then spread the water all over the head with one hand. At the start of a drumming session it is often a good custom to smudge yourself, the participants, the drum and the environment. Suitable herbs for this purpose are sage, sweetgrass, cedar, lavender or tobacco. Then it is also advisable to call the directions, offering smoke or invocations, and to officially open the Sacred Circle. The aim is to ground yourself and make sure that your body is anchored in the physical reality. This also involves sitting in a comfortable and empowering position. Keep your spine straight and breathe deeply using the full capacity of your lungs. Bring your attention to your breath and allow it to move to all parts of the body. Then let it extend to the drum and the stick that you are holding. Become one with the drum and its stick. Allow tensions to be released and find the right posture for you. Before drumming, I tend to remain silent for some time and connect with the Intent and Function. I listen to the beat of my heart and attune it to the drum. Once I have formulated my Intent and aligned it to the frequency of my heart, I invite the drum to carry its pulse as I start beating. As I proceed with my drumming I can allow the tempo to expand and change. At a certain stage I can also add my voice. Each sector and each Totem Spirit has its own rhythm and chant. Some of them belong to specific traditions, others are spontaneously produced in the moment in which they are played. The end of a drumming session is usually announced by a series of fast or slow beats. I generally conclude the drumming session by giving thanks for what has been received and closing the Sacred Circle.

The rattle is usually one of the first toys which is given to an infant. As the baby holds it in his hands and shakes it, he begins to perceive sounds and his capacity to interact with them. Rattles have been used in many cultures as powerful healing tools. Their shapes and sounds vary: some are like hail, rain, sea waves, others like thunder, the breaking up of ice or the crumbling of dry leaves. Rattles, as drums, can be employed to achieve shamanic states of consciousness. Their sound relaxes the mind and supports shamanic journeying. One of their functions is also that of breaking structures of rigidity and stagnation in the mind. In this sense they are tools that stimulate change and release of blocks. When the rattle is shaken and I pay attention to its sound, the resulting vibration spreads into the energy of my body, creating gaps and releasing grievances. Some shamans use it in this way to break models of attachment to illnesses and belief systems. Often the sound of the rattle can be used to identify critical areas that need attention. In this case the sound, for those who are able to perceive its variations, changes when it meets those zones. Then the shaman can provide healing by vigorously shaking the rattle over the critical areas.

The rattle is generally related to the energy of the Higher World and the positive, or male, polarity. When it is shaken, it draws the energy of the Higher and makes it available to be used according to the Intent of the operator. Rattles, along with drums, are also employed to open the Sacred Circle, because they are supposed to draw the attention of the Totem Spirits. The drum, being traditionally associated with the Earth, has a feminine nature and draws Earth energy toward the Higher. The combination of rattle and drum creates a complete energy circuit that facilitates the exchange between the Higher and the Lower Worlds.

Rattles are very simple tools that can either be purchased or made. Suitable material, if you decide to fabricate your own rattle, are gourds, coconuts, big shells, wood or carton boxes, old tin cans or plastic bottles, and a few beans, seeds, pieces of crystal, nails, sand, pebbles to place within. Another similar instrument is the *sistrum*, which generally consists of a small tree branch with a series of hanging objects (shells, twigs, pieces of metal) tied by a cord or attached to the branch itself. The *tambourine* is a very ancient instrument that combines the energy of the drum and the rattle. It is made up of a single-headed drum with pairs of metal cup-shaped discs inserted at intervals around the rim.

Please be aware that drums, rattles or any other instrument are not essential in shamanic work. This means that it is important to purchase or use them only if there is a sincere attraction and connection. The journey to find a drum or rattle is a sacred path. It does not matter if it takes time to get one. Holding the tension of not having one yet, often adds to the power and excitement of surrendering to the right moment in which a drum, if this is the case, will become available for me. As with all Sacred Tools, once you have purchased or received it, you should *activate* it through a ceremony of your choice and regularly take care of it. For example, you can offer smoke to your drum or rattle before and after every shamanic journey or ritual, and wrap it in a nice cloth when it is not in use.

Feathers

The presence of feathers as Sacred Tools is almost universal in shamanic traditions, as ubiquitous as the presence of birds all over this planet. Feathers are related to the power of ascension and descension in order to connect the Higher and the Lower Worlds. Their employment varies in different cultures: they can be used for purification; as a fan to direct and poke the smudging; for divination purposes; in massage practices; to balance the energy; as an anchor or protective device for shamanic journeys; as a sacred offering to evoke the medicine of a Spirit Animal or Totem Spirit; as accessories of other Sacred Tools (medicine shields, wands of power, etc.).

Feathers are generally associated with air signs or air sectors, although, according to the bird to which they belong, they also have correspondences with each of the Twelve Sectors. In this respect the feathers can be assembled in a special fan made up of twelve feathers (one for each bird of the Twelve Sectors). This object can be employed in the ritual practices of the Sacred Circle and used to connect the energies of the Twelve Sectors and direct them towards your Intent.

The Map of the Journey

This map is a representation of what you have seen or the messages you have received during shamanic journeys, visions, or dreams. No words are written on the map: only pictures, signs and drawings. This tool serves to remind of your experiences during shamanic journeys and can be employed in conjunction with the astroshamanic journal (see Chapter 5, 'The Astroshamanic Journal'), which is also a Sacred Tool. You can use a piece of white 100% cotton cloth, leather or paper of about 30 centimetres, or 12 inches square and divide it into 13 fields, each one representing a sector plus one for your Intent or Spirit Guide. You can also use an individual smaller map for each sector or adopt any other creative idea that inspires you. Upon concluding your shamanic exploration of a sector, the work on the map consists first of taking some time to skim through your notes, retrieving the most significant experiences, then drawing the field of the map corresponding to the sector involved. It does not matter if what you draw is not aesthetically beautiful. This is not a work of art. What counts is that it is meaningful for you. After you have drawn the field, write down some notes in your journal explaining your understanding of the picture.

Activation of Sacred Tools

When you find or buy a Sacred Tool it is advisable to do some activation work. There are different procedures according to different traditions and also for specific times of the year. Generally an ideal moment to activate Sacred Tools coincides with solstices, New or Full Moons and the passage of the Sun or Moon in the sector related to the tool. In astroshamanism the activation takes place mainly by consciously touching the tool while focussing on the Intent and Function. What follows is an example of activation:

1. Arrange the Sacred Circle using your Sacred Circle Pieces and place the tool you have decided to activate in the centre. If you like you can burn some herbs or incense and smudge the Circle and the tool.
2. Call upon your Spirit Guide and then focus the attention on your Intent for at least five minutes. Allow your body to become a representation of your Intent. Express and experience your Intent with all your senses. Connect your Intent to the Function and give permission to each sector to support you.
3. Bring your attention to the tool and place both your hands on it for some minutes, keeping the connection with your Intent and Function.
4. Blow seven times on the tool as a way to transmit your Intent. You can also let out a sound, chant, say some words or whatever can signify your Intent. Continue to touch the

object in all its parts and open up to receive a name for it. The first name that comes to you will be the right one.

5. Place the object in the centre of the Sacred Circle to indicate its connection with the Function. Stay in silence for some minutes and allow the tool to relate with the Circle.
6. If you wish you can conclude the activation with a dance, a chant or anything you feel drawn to do to welcome the tool and fully integrate it as part of your sacred equipment. Then close the Circle.
7. For at least one whole cycle of the Moon (28 days), touch the tool twice a day, calling it with its name and connecting with the Intent you expressed at the time of your first activation.

1 Spirit Medicines and Sacred Implanted Tools also contribute to the transformation and removal of other quite divergent and currently more prevalent implants. These devices are associated with Graha (see Chapter 7) and exist in most human physical, emotional and mental bodies. Their aim is to support the perception of separation and to block or disturb the connection with our Spirit Guide and true multi-dimensional nature.

2 Notes from teachings in *sacred idiom* translated and adapted by the author.

3 Please be aware that what is a power point for me is not necessarily one for everybody. It is the connection with my Spirit Circle (the shamanic power point) that determines the outer location of a power point, and not vice versa. According to my tradition, nobody is entitled to decide for others where a power point is located, unless he has been given direct consent by his tribe or community, or is strategically operating as the keeper of a specific tradition.

4 The Italian for *Ulysses*.

5 For this purpose a drumming tape or CD is also effective.

CHAPTER 9

ASTROSHAMANIC CHANTS, TRANCE POSTURES AND DANCES

Astroshamanic Chants

Chanting represents one of the most widespread and ancient religious practices of human beings. For ages shamans and multi-dimensional voyagers have used chants in order to connect with Spirit Guides and Totem Spirits or to achieve non-ordinary states of consciousness and journey into other realms. In astroshamanism chanting is employed to honour and connect with the various parts of the Sacred Circle and as a spiritual practice, where the body and the voice become a means through which Guides and Spirits can speak.

An astroshamanic chant has nothing to do with being in tune or in the right tempo according to the ordinary conventions of music. On the contrary there are times when such chants can sound like appalling screeches. Each chant is a unique sacred signature. It does not have to please a public or correspond to specific aesthetic canons. What matters here is to operate as a clear channel, so let go of judgements about how the voice should be and focus on lovingly releasing the energies which are transiting. When I chant my body becomes a device of communication with other dimensions and with my Spirit Guide or Circle. In this context I express all that cannot be conveyed through conventional language. This is a gigantic experience of communication that fully honours me and all my relationships at all levels. Chanting was a means of communication which existed long before the introduction of verbal languages. Through chanting I open the dialogue with ancient parts within me and re-establish my authentic original connection with other beings, animals, plants, minerals, planets and stars. This entails a quantum leap in communication and awareness which astroshamanic teachings suggest facing with adequate preparation, respect for natural cycles and careful integration.

The chants used in astroshamanism refer to three basic models of reference: the *System of the Planetary Chant,* the astroshamanic chants of the *Sacred Cone Circle* and the chants of the Earth-centred spiritual traditions based on the Sacred Circle.

The Planetary Chants, channelled by Andrew Ramer and introduced by Donna Cunningham,[1] consist of a series of sounds connected to the astrological planets. These chants have very ancient roots. Their function is that of sending out vibrations that allow the activation of high levels of energy. The effect is generally perceived as powerful, rebalancing and supportive of the integration of the characteristics associated with each planet.

The chants of the Earth-centred traditions come from many sources and carry the spirit of people and tribes who made chanting their religious practice.

The chants of the Sacred Cone Circle are the result of the connection with Totem Spirits and Spirit Guides. They come in different varieties: such as the popular ballads (*Trudeh Etnaie Korah*), the vulgar horizontal chants (*Seitoh Etnaie Korah*), the chants of release (*Grahe Korah*), the chants of the Totem Spirits and Guides (*Paheka Sadohe Korah*).

Some chants are transmitted by shamanic chanters or teachers in the ordinary reality and require initiatory procedures, while others belong to the heritage of the spiritual traditions of this planet and are easily accessible through tapes and books. Other chants emanate from unseen beings and other dimensions. They manifest spontaneously in the course of shamanic journeys or rituals and often are never repeated again, as they express the specific energy of that moment.

The sounds of chants in general can correspond either to words which are understandable by the ordinary human mind or to others that are totally unknown or *gibberish*. Usually the nature of the chant is so archaic and detached from current human conventions that it is impossible to translate it in any way. Although it can be stimulating for the mind, I suggest not indulging in the meaning of the words that are chanted. In most cases they are not words at all. Words are symbols that convey a meaning, whereas the sounds of shamanic chants are basically the significance itself. It is their vibrations that allow the transmission of information and induce a direct experience without the mediation of symbolic words. When I let my voice go, without any linguistic or musical censorship, I gradually release the layers that separate me from my original language and become transparent. Then I find the universal language of the heart that allows loving energy to be truly given away and shared. In this context, I dwell in the Middle World as the connecting agent between Higher and Lower Worlds. There I operate as channel, undisturbed by the energies that move through me, simply focusing on my Intent connected with the Function. As I allow this process to unfold, I need to be aware that my chants support a sacred transformational work that extends far beyond my human perception.

Chanting is not limited to ritual practices or environments and can be used any time it is required. When I feel depressed, afraid, bored, nervous, angry or in any other grieving mood, the turning point takes place the moment I take a deep breath, move into a dignified posture and let out the sound of my voice with the Intent of allowing the energy which is stuck to move.

A traditional way that I use for warming up before singing in a ritual context is the following. After smudging or cleansing myself, I open the Sacred Circle and then set my Intent connecting it with the Function. I close my eyes and bring my attention to the breath and heartbeat. Breath and heartbeat are the keys to all sounds. They constitute the basic communication shared by all physical living creatures. Breath and heartbeat connect us all. Their mutual interaction allows me to connect with my role as bridge between worlds. To activate this role, I allow my breath to circulate throughout my body as I listen to the rhythm of my heartbeat. In this process, I make sure that my upper chest as well as my belly are involved with breathing. When this happens breathing is more relaxed, as it receives the support from both the Higher and Lower Worlds. If I notice that my shoulders are raising, this may mean that I am not breathing with the belly. In this case I try again and continue until I am able to completely fill my lungs. Then I begin by toning some vowels: *ah, a, e, o, oo*. I open the mouth fully and exaggerate each vowel sound, using one complete out-breath for each vowel. Next I move to combinations of vowels: (*ao, au, eoo, ooah,* etc.) and combinations of vowels and consonants (*bah, be, boo, bo,* etc.). Vowels express the inner and pure energy of the word while consonants conduct that energy into a manifestation process that gives form to the outer reality.

Once I have attuned the major keys of my voice, and before starting the chant, I set the Intent. The Intent always has priority and is more important than the sound. Usually I repeat the Intent several times in the form of one or more sounds. For example, if I decide to receive guidance about my spiritual path on Earth, I chant the vowels of my name several times. This allows me to unite with the inner sacred purpose that my name conveys. By chanting the vowels of my surname, I connect with the deep motivation of my ancestral physical heritage, while using the vowels of spiritual names enables me to align with the roles I play within my spiritual and religious lineage. I can use the vowels of any name that is associated with my Intent (such as my community, business, partner, friend, town, tribe, car). According to my tradition, as long as vowels are used there is no risk of manipulating other people or situations. Therefore, unless I receive direct permission from the persons involved, I do not add the consonants. Vowels work at an inner level and draw the energy toward the shamanic form of what I perceive outside. This is in itself a major practice of healing as it allows me to release outer forms from my projections. To express my Intent I can also use any sound that I specifically receive for such a purpose. In this case, using the full words, including the consonants, is an essential part of the practice. As I add consonants, I activate the process of manifestation and notice how this contributes to grounding my Intent.

Another practice is that of projecting sounds in different parts of the body and in the areas linked with Sacred Tools (see Chapter 8, 'Sacred Tools'). In this case I employ the sounds of the vowels used at the beginning of the practice and choose various levels of intonation. Then I feel where in my body the sounds vibrate. I can also send some sounds toward specific parts (for example, left knee or forehead) and watch what happens. After this warm up, when I am ready, I can sing a complete chant. I let the chant flow freely from within. It can be a monotonous sound, a sequence of different phonemes that I repeat in cycles or one of the planetary and astroshamanic chants.

Chants of the Totem Spirits and Guides *(Paheka Sadohe Korah)*

These chants activate the energy field or consciousness represented by each sector and allow connection with its specific Totem Spirits and Auxiliary Guides. They have a strong effect, especially if they are done by a group. In the tradition of the Sacred Cone Circle each sector is identified with the name of a Totem Spirit. The energy of the sectors can be balanced, released, drawn and transformed by chanting the names of Totem Spirits and Guides. The traditional structure of such chants consists in repeating the name of a given Totem Spirit followed by the term *Sadoh*, which can be generally translated as 'Spirit Guide'. This combination is aimed at supporting the transformation of a Totem Spirit into a Spirit Guide. For example, the chant for the Totem Spirit of Sector 5 (*Surahim Tahe*) would be *Surahim Tahe Sadoh*. Please be aware that these names represent potent energies which need to be treated with respect. You are invited to use these chants only if you intend to establish or support a relationship with a specific Totem Spirit. The chant may be

The Twelve Sectors and Totem Spirits of the *Sacred Cone Circle*

Sector	Sign	Planet	Totem Spirit	Colour
1	Aries	Mars	Kahe Pahe	red
2	Taurus	Venus, Earth	Rata Sahe Pah	red-orange
3	Gemini	Mercury	Mahe Rahe Tahe	orange
4	Cancer	Moon	Quiushade	orange-yellow
5	Leo	Sun	Surahim Tahe	yellow
6	Virgo	Mercury, Asteroids	Kahesepoh Sadeh	yellow-green
7	Libra	Venus	Ataherah	green
8	Scorpio	Pluto, Mars	Harassadoah	green-blue
9	Sagittarius	Jupiter	Nivaya Sadhu	blue
10	Capricorn	Saturn	Sauter Kitaya	blue-violet
11	Aquarius	Uranus, Saturn	Uriah Tapeh	violet
12	Pisces	Neptune, Jupiter	Taepeh	violet-red

employed to accompany a shamanic journey of connection with the Totem Spirit involved. It can also be used as a practice on its own and in this case it is preferable to sing the chant once or twice a day for seven minutes for a period of 28 days.

A variation of the astroshamanic chants (*Paheka Rubhe Korah*) deals with the *Paheka Rubhe,* or *Binary Net of Totem Spirits,* i.e. the 144 combinations of the Twelve Totem Spirits,[2] and aims at releasing their grieving components. Here the first name of one Totem Spirit is combined with that of another followed by the term *Sadoh.* The Totem Spirit of a male (*Hare Paheka*) polarity precedes that of a female polarity (*Mare Paheka*). For example, the result of the union between *Hare Sauter Kitaya* (Hare Paheka of Sector 10) and *Mare Kahe Pahe* (Mare Paheka of Sector 1) is *Sauter Kahe Sadoh.* The final introduction of *Sadoh* signifies the acknowledgement of the *third party* created by the union and the release of the block of that specific binary net.

The System of the Planetary Scales

This system is an application of the Planetary Chants, which consist of a series of chants and colours associated with each astrological planet. Their effects manifest through the balancing and integration of the energy of the planet to which they refer. They also help release grievances, or difficult effects, of astrological aspects or transits. The aim of this system is to develop the capacity to move the energy from the lower to the higher expressions. The basic requirement of the scales consists of investing the maximum amount of energy at the lower levels. This means being available to face grievances and fears, to release them through the body and its sounds. Here you do not reach the *positive* by transcending or going beyond the negative, but by concentrating the energy at its lower levels and then moving it gradually to its higher levels. In this strategy it is essential to enter totally into the subtle essence of the lower frequencies. These are the ones that provide the energy that enables upward movement. For each scale, the chants are used in a specific structure made up of different stages. These stages refer to variations in tonality or distinct variations of energetic expressions in a gradual ascent from the lowest to the highest. The chant is employed in between each variation so as to facilitate the shift from one level to the other. During the practice of the scales, I sit still and allow images, emotions, thoughts and feelings to inwardly flow according to the content of each stage.

(See Table of Correspondences for the Planetary Scales, which provides lower and higher expressions associated with each planet.) If I prefer a more dynamic approach, I can use movement or dance.

The entire set of chants can be used regularly to integrate and harmonise the energies of all planets. In this regard, a heliocentric perspective is adopted. In this practice, the Sun is the starting point and corresponds to the body. After the chant of the Sun, from where the Intent emanates, I move to Mercury, perceived as a small planet orbiting a few centimetres from the body (the Sun). Venus is also very close, whereas the Earth and the Moon are about half a meter away, and so on until I reach Uranus, Neptune and Pluto, which are much farther away and can even be perceived as being out of the room.

Planetary Chants can be used whenever I need to manifest the energy of a planet or transform it into a higher vibration. They are tools at my disposal that I can employ in a large variety of ways. Once their basic function is honoured, there is ample space to be creative as regards their use.

The Table of the Planetary Chants

Planet	**Chant** (4 times)	**Chant** (closing)	**Colour**
Sun	Oh Hay Yah	Oh	bright red
Mercury	Oh Hi Ti Nah	Ti Oh	purple
Venus	Nah Ti Nah	Oh	bright green
Moon/ Earth	Si Idriah	Neh Hah Mah Set	white
Mars	Naizy Day Hoh Hi Mah	Kah Kah	black
Asteroids	Si Ti Yah Kah	Mah Si Kah *(when the chant is over, add* Ai Hey Poh)	mottled
Jupiter	Hi Su Mayo	Ay	yellow
Saturn	Dah Ti Kah	Oh Ay	brown
Chiron	Kah Si Mah	Kah	grey
Uranus	Nah Mitriah	Nah Simitri	silver
Neptune	Oh Myss	Oh	mint or sea green
Pluto	Ti Yah	Ah	clear glass or light wood

Table of Correspondences for the Planetary Scales		
Planet	**Grievances**	**Qualities**
Sun	Arrogance, boastfulness, hypocrisy, incompetence, indolence, inflexibility, jealousy, ostentation, pomposity, selfishness, tyranny, vanity.	Centring, creativity, dignity, generosity, joy, leadership, light, loyalty, play, power, pride, purpose, self-esteem, trust, vitality.
Mercury	Chattering, deceit. dishonesty, flightiness, intellectualism, nervousness, rationalisation, restlessness, scepticism, superficiality, trickery.	Awareness, communication, dexterity, discrimination, eloquence, fluency, humour, intelligence, understanding, versatility.
Venus	Avidity, co-dependency, compromise, indecision, indolence, jealousy, lustfulness, procrastination, projection, self-indulgence, sentimentality.	Art, balance, beauty, cheerfulness, co-operation, delight, grace, gratitude, harmony, love, peace, refinement, relationship, sharing.
Moon Earth	Attachment, clannishness, dependence, emotion/sex-addiction, laziness, materialism, moodiness, neediness, possessiveness, shyness.	Birth, growth, inclusiveness, intimacy, intuition, kindness, memory, pleasure, protection, receptivity, security, tenacity, tenderness, union.
Mars	Coarseness, competition, cruelty, destruction, impatience, irritability, rage, sadism, violence.	Boldness, clarity, courage, directness, dynamism, energy, initiative, self-reliance, spontaneity.
Asteroids	Criticism, fragmentation, fussiness, hyperactivity, perfectionism, work-addiction, worry.	Analysis, discrimination, efficiency, obedience, purification, precision, service, synthesis.
Jupiter	Dissipation, dogmatism, exaggeration, gambling, greed, over-eating, overoptimism, pretence.	Abundance, adventure, education, enthusiasm, faith, optimism, prosperity, trust, wisdom.

continued …

Planet	Grievances	Qualities
Saturn	Coldness, cynicism, depression, dullness, drudgery, fear, guilt, harshness, limitation, materialism, obstruction, pessimism, rigidity, sadness.	Authority, commitment, concentration, discipline, endurance, grounding, integrity, method, organisation, patience, reliability, responsibility.
Chiron	Illness, over-idealism, self-destruction, woundedness.	Healing, release, transformation, truth.
Uranus	Accidents, anarchy, chaos, destruction, eccentricity, extremism, licentiousness, perversion, rebellion, shocks, structurelessness, weirdness.	Brother-sisterhood, freedom, friendship, improvement, independence, inventiveness, quantum leap, renewal, synergy, synchronicity.
Neptune	Addictions, confusion, daydreaming, debauchery, deception, escapism, gullibility, hysteria, illusion, invisibility, spaciness, suicide, victimisation.	Compassion, devotion, empathy, gentleness, inspiration, intuition, mysticism, psychic ability, purity, sacrifice, spirituality, surrender, unity.
Pluto	The chant is used only for mourning and not for other expressions of Pluto.	

Planetary Rosaries

Planetary Rosaries are Sacred Tools representing the energy of a single planet or a combination of two planets and constitute a prominent application of Planetary Chants. Their function is to balance the effects of planetary aspects and transits or to transform the expression of a specific planet. The beads employed for Planetary Rosaries need to be of natural materials (wood, clay, stone, etc.) as does the thread (silk, cotton, leather, etc.) and dyes. The only exception here is Uranus, for which synthetic materials are preferable. When the rosary involves combinations of planets, it can only be made by somebody with the same type of pattern in his natal chart (i.e. as aspect, house–planet combination, etc.). For example, to build a rosary for Mars and Uranus one of the following pattern is required: an aspect between Mars and Uranus, Uranus in Aries, Uranus in the first house, Mars in Aquarius, Mars in the eleventh house. The ideal time for the preparation of a rosary can be during an aspect of the two planets, a related Sun–Moon combination (for example, in the previous case it would be Sun in Aries and Moon in Aquarius or Moon in Aries and Sun in Aquarius), a planetary day (see Chapter 10, 'Cycles of Time') or the transit of the Moon in one of the signs involved. The colours of the beads change according to planet and are given in the table which follows. (For associated colours see the Table of the Planetary Chants.)

A rosary is made by threading together two beads of the planet which is closer to the Sun, followed by one bead of the planet that is farther away. For example, in a Mars–Uranus rosary, two black beads are used for Mars (which is closer to the Sun than Uranus) and a silver one for Uranus. Similarly, in a Sun–Saturn rosary, two red beads are used for the Sun, followed by a brown one for Saturn. This system does not provide indications as regards the number of beads in the rosary. In the Buddhist and Hindu traditions rosaries are made of 108 beads (12 x 9). Shiva's rosaries have 32 or 64 beads, Christian rosaries have 165 or 60, while Muslim rosaries have 99 beads.

A good practice before threading the beads is that of focusing on the Intent. The beads of the two planets can be held in separate hands as the complete chant is sung: for example, with Sun–Saturn this would be *Oh Hay Yah, Oh Hay Yah, Oh Hay Yah, Oh Hay Yah, Oh* (Sun) and *Dah Ti Kah, Dah Ti Kah, Dah Ti Kah, Dah Ti Kah, Oh Ay* (Saturn). The beads are then threaded one by one, toning the first line of the planetary chant (*Oh Hay Yah* for the Sun and *Dah Ti Kah* for Saturn). Rosaries based on the energy of one specific planet can also be prepared. In this case only beads of that planet are employed.

Once the rosary is ready, the practice consists of chanting it once or twice a day for one to three cycles of the Moon, for the entire duration of the transit or until the desired results are achieved. The chant for a Sun–Saturn rosary would be *Oh Hay Yah* (first Sun bead), *Oh Hay Yah* (second Sun bead) *Dah Ti Kah* (Saturn bead) and so on until the end of the rosary is reached. The more the rosary is used, the more powerful it becomes. It can also be worn and used as a Sacred Tool or, once it has been employed for some time, given away to somebody with the same planetary dynamics at work.

Planetary rosaries are very powerful tools that allow greater awareness of the way in which planetary energies work in our lives. The fact that these energies are forced to live together in a rosary creates an exposure of the related grievances and their transformation. This process, once it is accepted and acknowledged, can bring about a rebalancing and actualisation of the luminous potential of the planets involved.

Planetary rosaries are practical strategies to create a dialogue with the sectors of the Sacred Circle, with Totem Spirits, Guides and planets, allowing them to operate and us to learn to listen to what they have to say. These energies were once directly accessible on this planet, then due to the reduction of human perception, they were projected onto the planets and constellations in the Sky, along with the highest dream of mankind. The chants are just one among the many tools that facilitate the return to the original awareness and dignity of all living beings.

Shamanic Trance Postures

From ancient times we have inherited statues, carvings, paintings and various ornaments that, far from being artistic or creative expressions of the culture of those epochs, constitute actual learning devices for achieving connections with other dimensions. These figures portray men or women in specific positions which allow access to altered states of consciousness. The artifacts revealing these postures can be found in the most ancient traditions all over the world. The anthropologist Felicitas D. Goodman has carried out extensive research on the topic. Since 1977 she has studied more than 50 postures that facilitate the receipt of significant visions and a direct experience of the oldest myths of humankind.[3] The characteristic of these and other postures is that each one of them is in itself a portal that unseals the perception of other dimensions.

This type of contact, together with nomadism, hunting and spontaneous collection of food, seems to have been a main feature of the people who inhabited the Earth up to 40,000 years ago. An idea of what life could have been like in those times has been documented by some contemporary anthropologists and researchers who have managed to spend time with the few native peoples who have continued to keep their tradition unaltered.[4] The life of those generations, technically called *hunter gatherers*, 'is characterised by balance and harmony with the natural world – not just with animals but with all life forms, including wind and thunder, rocks and insects. Humans are not thought of as having dominion over the Earth or any of its inhabitants, and so gathering hunters are not focused on attempts to control their environment, but rather on living in harmonious relationship with the seasons, the elements, and all living beings. This attitude is so effective and adaptive that gathering and hunting existed as the only way of life on our planet for thousand of years.'[5] For many and still unexplained reasons the prevalence of such attitudes decayed and new societies devoted to the cultivation of plants and breeding of animals prevailed. Human beings started to concentrate their energies within limited territories and avoided nomadism, for they needed to stay close to their farms and control the cycles of nature. Social life began to change and during this process human beings seemed to lose that sense of deep connection with nature which was typical of their ancestors. In their spiritual practices, however, these people continued to keep the link with non-ordinary realities and with the experiences of previous cultures. Through the metamorphosis activated by trance states 'it was possible to soften the boundaries between humans, animals, and plants. The use of ritual body postures was developed within horticultural societies. These were the people who refined the use of body postures as rituals that gave shape to religious trance. Dr. Goodman discovered that they passed along to us a well-defined system that teaches us how to enter Alternate Reality, the spirit world, where we can return to a state of harmony with the four-legged, those that fly, those that swim, the plants, the trees, and the rocks.'[6]

To employ the postures it is useful to consider a few simple suggestions. It is like operating a computer programme. According to the key which is pressed different effects are possible. This means that it is important to assume the right position and also to be aware of the different results that each position can produce. The main feature of the postures is that they are authentic ritual ceremonies that express themselves through a static position. The ritual is aimed at establishing a connection with other dimensions and going beyond the ordinary state of perception.

To practise the postures it is necessary to employ the auditory stimulation of the rattle or drum. All the basic precautions and suggestions used for any shamanic journey are valid here as well. Felicitas Goodman suggests focusing on the breath and doing 50 full breaths before starting the posture. This practice of counting 50 breaths is an ideal preparation and allows the release of whatever is distracting. Then the position is assumed and the rattle or drum starts. During the time that follows, the only task is to remain in the correct position and to be open to the experience that develops. If you lose concentration or space out, bring the focus of attention to the rhythmic sound. 'Trance is not always the same. You may feel a change in your body temperature, find yourself rocking or swaying, or experience energy flowing through parts of your body. You may see patterns of color or witness complex visions that resemble watching a movie. Sometimes you may hear sounds or voices; if you find yourself interacting with an animal or other spirit, you may ask questions and receive answers. Occasionally, people even report smelling specific aromas.'[7] The practice usually lasts 15 minutes and at the end you can use the customary procedure employed for bringing any shamanic journey to a close. It is useful to write down the major features of the experience or to do a drawing. This is important even if nothing apparently seems to have happened.

Astroshamanic totemic postures are applications of shamanic trance postures used in the context of astroshamanism to connect with the Totem Spirit of each sector. These postures are derived from the icons depicted at the beginning of each chapter on the sectors in the second book.

Astroshamanic Dance

In ancient times dance was neither a form of artistic expression performed by a bunch of experts nor a performance of athletic and technical prowess. It was used as a tool to achieve a state of ecstasy where the dancer, letting go of his false perception as a separated unit, would uncover his true nature and surrender to the guidance of Spirit. The whole point of such dance consists of releasing the identification with the ego and thoroughly experiencing a multi-dimensional enlargement of consciousness. The techniques and the conditions used to achieve this are irrelevant. What counts is to reach a stage where I do not regard myself anymore as a piece of flesh manipulated by an invented ego identity. Here I move beyond the fiction of my boundaries and bridge into the essential vibration of ecstatic reality. Yet, as I am possessed by this blissful energy, things still continue to proceed around me. I remain aware of my environment and simply look at it as a witness, firmly grounded in my connection with the Guide. This way of dancing is available to anybody who sincerely wishes to transit from the hallucination of separation to the true perception of unity. Anyone who is capable of moving at least one bone of his body is in the right condition to dance. It is an inner operation, devoid of any purpose of public performance, aimed at revealing experiences and visions beyond time and space. 'Make it a point to simply dance to God. So there is no need to be technical – because He is not an examiner. You will simply dance as a small child... as a prayer. Then dance will have a totally different quality to it. You will feel for the first time that you are taking steps that you have never taken before; that you are moving in dimensions which have never been known to you. Unfamiliar and unknown ground will be traversed.'[8]

In astroshamanism, through dance I invite the energy of the sectors to be with me and assist me in retrieving all the lost pieces of who I truly am. Each Totem Spirit and every zodiacal sign has its own frequency and through dance I can align to its modalities of expression and incorporate them in the expansion of my identity. Here I open myself to Totem Spirits, stars, planets, and whatever exists around me, asking to reactivate the memory of my ancient communion with them. By physically dancing the Sectors, I enter into their rhythm, experiencing their energies and directing them toward my highest Intent. It is one of the most powerful ways to connect Earth and Heaven, matter and spirit, *Rodnah* and *Handor*, and release the patterns of astrological aspects and transits which obscure my perception.

Astroshamanic dance is a powerful catarthic practice that can be effectively used as a method for astroshamanic journeys. This means that I can do all the astroshamanic routine practices (i.e. meeting the Guide, exploring the sectors, connecting with Totem Spirits, receiving Spirit Medicines, etc.) by using dance and movements, instead of sitting or lying down. When using dance for such a purpose the same care and precautions applied as in other shamanic journeys and rituals are to be observed. Before starting the dance, remain still for some minutes, standing with your feet parallel to your shoulders and breathing deeply. Proclaim your Intent, call upon your Guide and, if you wish, invite the energy of a specific sector or Totem Spirit to dance with you. Eyes are kept closed or covered with a blindfold. You can employ a shamanic drumming or rattling tape or specific monotonous music. When the music starts, gently align your body to the rhythm and gradually let it go freely. Allow your astroshamanic journey to resonate through the movements of your body. If you are exploring a specific sector, open up to its energy and invite it to employ your body as a vehicle. At the end of the dance (which could last from 20 to 45 minutes), be still for at least 5 minutes and take time to silently integrate your experience. Then, as usual, write down or draw your observations and insights in your journal.

It is important to be aware that astroshamanic dance, besides being intended as a ritual or shamanic journey, also works as a practice of release. In this context, I offer my energy through the physical movement and the total participation of all other bodies (emotional, mental, spiritual). I give what I am channelling in that particular moment (excitement, vitality, pain, weakness, restlessness, sexual energy, craziness) until a void is created. This will constitute the space for receiving. Having relinquished what is in excess, I am then ready to receive the gifts which are necessary for my healing and transformation.

Various music and sounds can be employed to accompany the dance. Monotonous sounds (such as drumming, rattling, waves) are ideal as they do not influence or interfere with the experience of the dancer. Dance can also take place with no external sound at all. In this case the subject is invited to listen to his own internal music or to use his own body as a musical instrument (stamping the feet, clapping, breathing out and in). Rhythmic or melodic sounds are helpful when, on the contrary, the intent is to evoke or attract a specific energy or experience.

1 Donna Cunningham, *Astrology and Spiritual Development*, Cassandra Press, 1989, pp. 105–116.

2 See Chapter 2, note 7.

3 See: Felicitas D. Goodman, *Where the Spirits Ride the Wind: Trance Journeys and Other Ecstatic Experiences*, Indiana University Press, 1990. Belinda Gore, *Ecstatic Body Postures: An Alternate Reality Workbook*, Bear & Company, 1995. Franco Santoro, 'Le posture estatiche di trance sciamanica' in *Alpha Dimensione Vita*, Anno III – N. 18.

4 For example: Richard Katz, *Boiling Energy: Community Healing Among the Kalahari Kung,* Harvard University Press, 1982; Marlo Morgan, *Mutant Message Downunder,* MM Co., 1991.

5 Gore, *Ecstatic Body Postures,* pp. 14–15.

6 Gore, Ibid. pp. 17–18.

7 Gore, Ibid. p. 35.

8 Osho, *The Orange Book: the Meditation Techniques of Bhagwan Shree Rajneesh,* Rajneesh Foundation, 1983, p. 8. (This book, which contains a wide range of meditation techniques and precious insights, is out of print and is currently replaced by Osho, *Meditation: The First and Last Freedom,* St. Martin's Press, New York, 1996.)

CHAPTER 10

THE ASTROLOGICAL LANGUAGE

Astrology is a tool aimed at interpreting reality through a symbolic and strategic structure. The natal chart, the human psyche, the material world, all are mere symbols. This means that they are external, or seen, forms through which I can perceive an inner, or unseen, meaning. The planets, the universe and all human beings exist at a physical level, yet beyond this context they have other multi-dimensional natures and a spiritual essence. The symbolic key is properly at work when I manage to perceive this spiritual essence out of the external, or material, form. Transformation, meant as healing, integration or expansion of awareness, takes place when I establish a rapport with what lies beyond the symbolic form and have a direct experience of the spiritual energy and of its unity with whatever exists. In order to use astrology in this process I need to perceive the natal chart as a reflection of the totality of the inner and outer world, or of shamanic and ordinary states of consciousness, and also to use tools that allow me to relate to its various components.

Apart from what I think is in best interests of myself or others, my authentic nature is connected with a specific Intent that is the foundation of my true potential and that triggers the Function which brought me here. During life this Intent develops through various stages of transformation and key events that are fully relevant to my higher self, or Spirit Guide, although they may be difficult to understand for the ordinary personality. The advantage of astrology lies in providing a codified language able to identify and define some of the basic components and dynamics of human existence. This language, when examined through my inner experience, can allow me to obtain a wider and clearer vision as regards the direction of my cycles. In brief, astrology offers the possibility of understanding the energies at play and the opportunity of identifying, not only the modalities, but also the specific times in which they express and transform themselves during my life.

The development of astrology dates back to the first appearance of human beings on Earth and has been developing ever since. The need to communicate with other human beings produced a series of gestures and sounds that was later translated into specific alphabetic languages. The need to transmit deeper meanings and to relate with invisible forces determined the birth and the successive development of the astrological language.

In astroshamanism I employ the astrological language in its essential features as a strategic analytical grid for the work with the Sacred Circle. In this context it is not necessary to consider the numerous techniques and methods of interpretation on which astrological literature thrives. The essence of astrological language is extremely simple. Its applications can become unnecessarily complex. And here it is important to be clear about what I want to do with this language, or what my Intent is. For example, if I want to write a text on a computer, I just need to know how to use the word processor programme and this will suffice to complete my task. I do not need to study other features of the programme, the software for graphics and algebraic calculations or the internal functioning of the word processor, not to mention the hardware. What counts is to manifest my Intent of writing a text. Then, in my spare time, if this really interests me, I can decide to learn more about the computer and its further functions

In astroshamanic work the use of astrology allows me to identify and define the decisive passages of individual and collective existence. In this way it is possible to understand the relevant energies of a given situation and its relationship with past events or future potentials. Here I need to use extreme caution so as not to use these tools in an improper way and interfere with the authentic development of the experience.

Astrological language and techniques are not dealt with directly in this text. The majority of this information is widely available in many books. In this chapter my aim is to provide a brief description of astrological language and some of its application in astroshamanism. You can find specific details about astrological signs, houses and planets in the second book.

Traditional Astrological Correspondences of the Twelve Sectors

Sector	Planet	House	Sign	Element	Quality	Polarity
1	Mars	First	Aries	Fire	Cardinal	Positive
2	Venus	Second	Taurus	Earth	Fixed	Negative
3	Mercury	Third	Gemini	Air	Mutable	Positive
4	Moon	Fourth	Cancer	Water	Cardinal	Negative
5	Sun	Fifth	Leo	Fire	Fixed	Positive
6	Mercury	Sixth	Virgo	Earth	Mutable	Negative
7	Venus	Seventh	Libra	Air	Cardinal	Positive
8	Pluto	Eighth	Scorpio	Water	Fixed	Negative
9	Jupiter	Ninth	Sagittarius	Fire	Mutable	Positive
10	Saturn	Tenth	Capricorn	Earth	Cardinal	Negative
11	Uranus	Eleventh	Aquarius	Air	Fixed	Positive
12	Neptune	Twelfth	Pisces	Water	Mutable	Negative

The Twelve-Letter Alphabet

All aspects of life, according to astrology, can briefly be reduced to Twelve Sectors, or ways of being. The astrological language is therefore an alphabet with twelve letters.[1] An alphabet can be printed in capital, small or bold letters and with various fonts, yet a 'Z' conveys the same principle of a 'z' or '*z*'. Similarly, in astrology, the Twelve Sectors, or twelve basic letters, can be represented through different expressions of the same alphabet. Some of them play a major role (planets, houses and signs); others have minor features (for example, decanates, fixed stars, dwadashamsa).

Each zodiac sign is associated with an astrological house: the first sign (Aries) with the first house, the second (Taurus) with the second house, etc. These houses and signs have the same principle, or sector, in common. At the same time, each planet is related with the general principle of a house or sign. Here some incongruities may arise as there are twelve houses and twelve signs, whereas the astrological planets (comprising also the Sun and the Moon) are traditionally ten. The problem strategically ceases to exist once I am aware that some planets have a double function. Just as in the English language the alphabetical symbols C and G correspond to different sounds (for example, in words like *car* and *centre* or *garden* and *gentle*), the planet Mercury coincides with both Gemini/third house and Virgo/sixth house, whereas the planet Venus relates both with Taurus/second house and Libra/seventh house. Certain astrological approaches do not limit themselves to the ten planets and employ other celestial bodies corresponding to principles that do not find a complete definition in the traditional alphabet, as for example the asteroids and planet Earth. According to the model of the Twelve Sectors, signs, houses and planets represent the same basic principle. This does not mean that they are the same.

The structure of the twelve-letter alphabet shows that the various combinations of astrological language (planets, houses, signs, etc.) share twelve basic themes. 'Astrology deals with twelve basic ways of being in the world, twelve fundamental human drives, twelve human needs and modes of operation. Each of the twelve is positive – no malefic. Each of the twelve is necessary – a part of being human. Each of the twelve if overdone, or expressed to the exclusion of any of the other eleven – can be destructive. These twelve sides of life are mirrored in the horoscope by a planet, a house and a sign.'[2] For example, Sector, or letter, 3 refers to the planet Mercury, the third house and the sign Gemini. In this system we can briefly define the planets as the chief factors and the most emphatic forms of astrological language. They identify the energy in its essential form: the different visages of God, the master roads that allow access to the Centre, the basic archetypes, the Totem Spirits. They are the *what?* of astrological grammar. The houses represent the *where?*: the specific fields of experience where the energies of the planets express themselves. In the houses the nature and the specialisation of an individual is depicted. The signs relate to the modalities of expression of the planetary energies. They represent the *how?*

The zodiac signs are the most popular feature in astrology and generally relate to consensus reality, tribal consciousness and the basic social identifications of human beings. They refer to the mental and objective plane, and differ from the energetic and subjective character of the planets. In astroshamanism zodiac signs belong to the periphery of the Sacred Circle and express less evolved qualities related to Level 1. At the same time, signs have a primary importance as they indicate the beginning of the transformational path and the way of return toward the Centre of the Sacred Circle. The twelve astrological signs constitute the access to three levels. Marcus Allen defines them as *unevolved, evolutive,* and *evoluted.* 'Each sign is a sign of transformation... The unevolved is the "ground", or starting point... The evolving is the "path", or direction of growth... The evolved is the "goal", or the fruit of the search. [...] The evolving qualities use the same energies as the unevolved qualities of each sign – but they are used in conscious, creative, useful ways which lead to growth, to health, and to the dissolving of limitations. The very "negative" emotions themselves provide the energy which causes transformation into a higher state of being... The unevolved qualities of each sign are the same thing as the evolved qualities – it is all energy ... the only difference is the level of vibration. Our very weaknesses give us the strength for growth.'[3]

The zodiac signs have nothing to do with the constellations which bear the same name. They do not have the same size as, although before the Christian era signs and constellations appeared to coincide, the precession of the equinox has since then produced a separation of approximately 30° to the right of the constellations with the same name as the signs. Zodiac signs are traditionally divided in three groups: *elements, qualities* and *polarities.* The elements, or *triplicities* (so-called as each element consists of three zodiac signs), include Fire, Earth, Air and Water. The nature of each of these elements defines many features of their related signs, although each one of them has a different expression. Qualities, or *quadruplicities* (so named because each one of them consists of four zodiac signs), are *cardinal, fixed* and *mutable.* They represent the kind of vibration through which the elements express themselves. Cardinal signs (Aries, Cancer, Libra, Capricorn) correspond to direct energy, action, dynamism, opening of new phases and seasonal starts. Fixed signs (Taurus, Leo, Scorpio, Aquarius) refer to concentration of energy, to the grounding of the preceding phase and the seasonal climax. Mutable signs (Gemini, Virgo, Sagittarius, Pisces) represent the transition toward change, the passage of the spiral movement, and the end of the season. Cardinal, fixed and mutable signs also astroshamanically relate with the Higher, Lower and Middle World respectively. The combination of the four elements with the three qualities produces the twelve zodiac signs. Polarities are *positive* and *negative,* or *male* and *female.* Fire and air signs belong to the positive polarity, whereas water and earth signs to the negative.

The astrological houses are a lesser known element in astrology and generally refer to individual consciousness. They represent the specific areas of experience in which the planetary energies tend to operate. They refer to the *where?*

Planets are the most emphatic and relevant form of the astrological alphabet and are associated with cosmic consciousness. They represent the *what?* In the astrological language there are two kinds of planets which are often defined as *personal* and *transpersonal.* The latter are represented by Uranus, Neptune and Pluto. These planets were discovered in recent times and are not part of traditional astrology developed over the past 2000 years. They relate to multi-dimensional experiences that do not belong to the ordinary structure of the ego and are often associated with different kinds of trance states. Personal planets feature the Sun, Moon, Mercury, Venus, Mars, Jupiter and Saturn. They represent the ordinary ingredient of the ego structure and tend to be easily integrated in ordinary life. The planetoid Chiron is regarded by some astrologers as the bridge between personal and transpersonal planets.

Together with planets, signs, houses, elements, qualities and polarities there are also other linguistic factors derived from the same combinations of planets, houses and signs. Their function is to allow the actual functioning of the astrological language. If planets, as we have seen, are considered the main factor, their angular relations (*aspects* and *transits*) play a role of major importance. They define the quality of the relationship and the level of interaction between planets. The expression of a planet can change enormously according to the house or sign where it is positioned, and its proximity to *angles* or *midpoints* of angles.

The Astrological Map

The astrological map, or natal chart, is a code representation of the Sky based on a specific moment and place of observation. In ancient times these maps were compiled through observation and direct experience of the Sky and the Earth. They considered, besides the positions of celestial bodies, further information like atmospheric phenomena, the colour and shape of the Moon and the Sun, the clouds and landscape, the presence of certain animals, plants, sounds, visions and dreams. Nothing was neglected, as humans were seen as part of the whole and there was no separation between the Sky and the Earth. Then this attitude began to disintegrate. Direct observation was limited to the Sky and became so complex that only a few experts could deal with it. It was then that the separation intensified and put in place the foundations for most of the cultures we have inherited from our recent ancestors.

Nowadays, in order to obtain the data necessary for their work, astrologers employ specific books (such as the *Ephemeris* and *Tables of Houses*) or computer programs. In the natal chart the positions of celestial longitudes of the astrological planets and other points of reference (houses, nodes, midpoints, etc.) are indicated as they were for the time and place of an individual's birth.

The astrological map, similarly to a photograph, is the *freezing* of a movement. In this case it is that of the Sky and the Earth: the widest movement that human beings can conceive. The freezing of this motion perfectly describes the hallucination of the ego. The energy was flowing undisturbed and at a certain point it halted giving rise to a condensed form that the astrological map portrays in its multiple aspects. The celestial bodies and the Earth have actually never arrested their motion and have always continued their journey. Yet the ego is glued there still and it is with that frozen moment that it persists in identifying itself. This identity, anchored to the arrest of a past instant, makes us live in a *separate reality* of which we are both victims and creators. It is a hallucination that remain more or less undisturbed until, in certain moments in life, we come to terms with the present reality and the actual movement of the energy in the Sky and on the Earth. In those moments, which astrology calls *transits*, the temperature rises and ice thaws uncovering the precariousness of our frozen state. These are often major occasions when it is possible to open a gap and bring to light something more about the mystery of the life that surrounds us. Due to the transformative effects on our structure of identity, transits may also coincide with considerable times of crisis.

The astrological map indicates what I am in relation to what I have thought and done in the past. It provides a portrait of the blocks that I have created in the course of my existence. This freezing obstructs true perception and continues to keep me in a dimension of limited experience. Certain traditions teach that men reincarnate continually due to the attachment to their grievances. In this sense the natal chart provides a picture of all my major blocks and of what I need to release. Traditional astrology generally considers the natal chart in linear term as something that needs to be evolved. If I am born, for example, with Sun in Virgo, then my purpose is to achieve my full potential as a Virgo. From another perspective, if I am born Virgo it means that there are specific grievances in Virgo that I am here to acknowledge, release and transform. This does not mean that I will not fulfil the potentials of Virgo, but that I am here to move beyond Virgo, to unfreeze it.

The natal chart is the result of a complex series of astronomical calculations and consists of an arrangement of various symbolic signs, i.e. the astrological alphabet. It is not essential to understand immediately all the information contained in the natal chart. Its significant messages will reveal themselves according to circumstances and in a way which is experientially understandable for you.

Angles and Midpoints

Angles are the cusps, or starting lines, of the first, seventh, fourth and tenth house and correspond to Ascendant, Descendant, Immum Coeli and Medium Coeli respectively. Astroshamanically they refer to the Four Directions of the Sacred Circle (East, West, South, North), the two poles of the horizontal axis, or Middle World (Ascendant and Descendant), and of the vertical axis (Immum Coeli as Lower World, and Medium Coeli as Higher World).[4] These positions are generally considered the most sensitive points of the natal chart so that a planet which is in close aspect to them has a strong influence in the life of the person concerned. *Midpoints* of angles are found midway between one angle and the other, and correspond to the four secondary directions (South-West, North-West, North-East, South-East). These positions refer to the areas where the ego sense of separation is dominant and, sooner or later, faces a crisis. Here the individual is at times confronted with some of the major blocks on his path of transformation. Such situations play an important role as, although they may appear painful, they force a choice between the illusion of the identification with the ego and the reality of unity of our spiritual nature. This characteristic of midpoints is exemplified by the fact that in the traditional versions of the Sacred Circle, the secondary directions, as distinct from the Four Directions, do not have paths of self-realisation leading towards the Centre. The advantage of midpoints is that they expose the block and the impossibility of moving farther toward the Centre unless there is a conscious choice of direction.

Planetary Aspects

For each individual, every planet has a modality of expression which differs according to the position it occupies in the astrological map at the moment of birth (the still photograph) and to its successive movements (the continuation of the film). These diversities of expression are identified by computing the angular separation between planets or other astrological points. The distances which are considered significant take the name of *aspects*. The aspects that refer to the natal position are called *natal aspects*. Those which regard the relationship between the natal positions and the successive movements of the planets are named *transits*. Aspects define the type of relationship that exists between two or more planets or astrological points and the way in which they tend to function in the areas described by the astrological map. Aspects are based upon fractional divisions of the 360° circle of the ecliptic. The main aspects are the following:

Table of Planetary Aspects

Symbol	Aspect	Distance	Orb*	Effects
☌	Con-junction	0°	8–10°	Unity, initiative. Easy, depending on the planets involved.
☍	Opposition	180°	8–10°	Polarity, confrontation, projection, conflict. Very energetic.
△	Trine	120°	6–8°	Harmony, integration, motivation, delight, fluidity, stability. Very easy.
□	Square	90°	8–10°	Challenge, effort, block, resistance. Very energetic.
⚹	Sextile	60°	4–6°	Efficiency, productivity, opportunity, automatism. Easy.
Q	Quintile	72°	3°	Strength, creativity, talent. Easy.
⚻	Quincunx	150°	2–4°	Effort, realisation, aspiration. Energetic.
II	Parallel	0°	1°	Unity. Easy.

* The orb is the distance in degrees within which an aspect is considered to be effective.

Basically, there are two types of aspects: those traditionally regarded as *easy* and those considered *difficult*. Easy aspects indicate that among the parts involved there is a spontaneous and easy interaction, whereas difficult aspects, that I prefer to call *energetic*, indicate a certain tension or concentration of energy capable of producing either the most consistent grievances or significant blessings.

When two planets are in an energetic aspect they tend to manifest the main situations of forgiveness and transformation in my life. It is with them that confrontation and challenges are likely to occur during astroshamanic journeys. With the help of the Guide, I can establish a dialogue with planets, in the form of Totem Spirits, to get to know the actual state of their conditions and what causes them to create problems.

Each situation of grievance or crisis has a specific reason and derives from a wrong communication between two or more forces. Here I have the chance of taking responsibility and claiming my power. Through the Guide, I can summon conflicting or grieving planetary forces. I can tell them that when they refuse to cooperate and comply with my highest Intent, they contribute to create pain and havoc in my life and in those who surround me. This dialogue involves asking what they need from each other and me in order to create harmony and constructive co-operation.

When two planets are in easy aspect they possess a spontaneous disposition to operate together and creatively unite their energies. They are seldom in conflict, although they can often cause conditions of inertia and automatism, when the Intent is confused or separated from the Function. The forces linked by easy aspects may at times have such a good time together that, if they are not consciously acknowledged or the environment is not ideal and the person lacks any Intent, they can decide to do their own business or serve the purpose of other people, entities or situations who have a clear Intent. When this happens, both with easy and energetic aspects, it is a question of retrieving these forces with the help of the Guide or suitable allies, finding out what were the causes that brought about the separation and making the necessary adjustments. By using the natal chart and various techniques of shamanic journey or *soul retrieval*, we can identify these forces and ask or give clarification in order for them to contribute to our Intent connected to the Function.

Planetary Roles

Planets play different roles according to their placement in the natal chart. These roles determine the conditions and the balances of power among the Totem Spirits. In astroshamanism we consider three principal roles (*ruler, regent, transiting*) and a series of accessory roles that I am now going to describe briefly.

The *ruler* is the equivalent of the Totem Spirit and represents the higher authority of each sector. Astrologically it is the planet that is most associated with the characteristics of a given sign or house (see Table of Planetary Dignities and Debilities, overleaf). The role of predominance on its related Sector is such in all circumstances and for all individuals. For example, the Moon (Spirit of Sector 4) is always the ruler of the sign of Cancer and the fourth house even if in an individual's chart the Moon is in another sign or house. Since the discovery of Uranus, Neptune and Pluto, there have been some changes in planetary rulerships so that certain signs (Aquarius, Pisces and Scorpio) have a new and an old ruler.

The *regent* refers instead to the specific position of the planet in the natal chart and therefore changes according to each individual. For instance, if a person was born with Saturn in Cancer or in the fourth house, the regent planet of that sign or house will be Saturn. A sign or a house can also have more than one regent planet or none at all. The roles of power of a *regent* planet vary according to its position and relationships with other planets. The traditional system of *planetary dignities and debilities* (see Table of Planetary Dignities and Debilities, overleaf) provides a general overview. A planet that is regent in the sign or house where it is also ruler is in harmony with the characteristics of that sign or house and generally expresses its power with great ease. A planet in *exaltation* is also in a relevant position. When a planet is in the sign opposite its rulership, it is said to be in *exile* or *detriment*. In this case its functioning may not be easy when ordinary expressions are concerned. The tendency could be that of causing conflicts and tensions or requiring large amounts of energy. On the other hand, if the Intent of the person involved is clear and connected with the Function, its power can exceed that of the ruling planet. A planet is in *fall* when is positioned in the sign opposite to its exaltation. Conventionally, this position is not ideal to the nature of the planet which may be debilitated or limited in its expression. It tends to produce high quantities of energy which can easily cause blocks and grievances. Similarly to the exile, this condition becomes an element of advantage when the energy is consciously directed.

A planet is *transiting* in that given period of time when it passes through a zodiac sign or house. This role may apply individually or collectively. At the time I am writing, for example, Neptune is in Aquarius and is therefore for each individual the transiting planet of that sign. As regards the houses, the situation changes according to each individual. If in my natal chart the area of the sign of Aquarius, where Neptune is transiting, corresponds to the fourth house, then it means that this is its transiting planet.

An additional feature is given by the planets in the role of *dispositor* that include both the regent planets situated in their ruling signs and the planets in *mutual reception* (a pair of planets mutually posited in each other's sign of rulership). The ruler of a sign is the *dispositor* of any planet situated in the sign that it rules. For example, if Uranus is in Leo, the Sun is its dispositor, for the Sun rules the sign of Leo; if Mars is in Cancer, the Moon is its dispositor, for the Moon rules the sign of Cancer. The premise is that when a planet is placed in a sign that is ruled by another planet, it is supposed to offer its services or act in ways that are influenced by its dispositor (i.e. the planet that rules the sign). In astroshamanic terms, any problem or comfort you experience with the Totem Spirit of a specific planet may be connected with its own dispositor, and vice versa. Since the two Totem Spirits have a direct link, it is also possible to turn to one of them in order to ease or heal issues related to the other.

Opposite is a table with the traditional description of these factors, together with the recent allocation given to planets beyond Saturn.

Cycles of Time

One of the most typical features of astrology and its application to astroshamanism regards its capacity to define the characteristics and the energetic nature of a specific moment in time. I am part of a great cosmic whole where things move at different levels and cycles. To acknowledge these cycles allows me to gradually harmonise my life with those of other beings and expand my identification. Astroshamanism is a way of fostering an increased experiential awareness of the energy changes that can be strategically and astrologically measured. In traditional spiritual astrology, in order to perform certain actions or

Table of Planetary Dignities and Debilities

Sign	Rulership	Exaltation	Exile	Fall
Aries	Mars	Sun	Venus	Saturn
Taurus	Venus	Moon	Pluto, Mars	Uranus
Gemini	Mercury		Jupiter	
Cancer	Moon	Jupiter	Saturn	Mars
Leo	Sun	Pluto	Uranus, Saturn	
Virgo	Mercury	Mercury	Neptune, Jupiter	Venus
Libra	Venus	Saturn	Mars	Sun
Scorpio	Pluto, Mars	Uranus	Venus	Moon
Sagittarius	Jupiter		Mercury	
Capricorn	Saturn	Mars	Moon	Jupiter, Neptune
Aquarius	Uranus, Saturn		Sun	Pluto
Pisces	Neptune, Jupiter	Venus	Mercury	Mercury

When a second planet is mentioned it refers to the old system of rulerships.

practices, specific times are considered suitable or non suitable. In the past it was essential to perform rituals or certain operations only on particular days. If this requirement fell short there was no point in doing anything. As far as I am concerned the first conditions consist in being clear about the nature of the Intent and connecting it with the Function. When this clarity is strong, all other considerations become less relevant.

An effective method to connect with the energy of a sector is that of being aware of the position of the Moon in each sign. During the course of 27 days and 12 hours, the Moon makes a complete revolution around the Zodiac and transits in each signs. Therefore, for example, when the Moon is in Aries, it is easier to connect with Sector 1, especially at a physical and emotional level. In this case the Moon tends to stir grievances blocked in the past for the purpose of releasing. The position of the Sun creates the counterpart relation and activates the Binary

Net of the Totem Spirits (*Paheka Rubhe*).[5] The lunar phase (angular distance between Sun and Moon) will provide other clues, together with the position of all other planets.

A method typical of the western esoteric traditions is that of the planetary days and hours. This involves choosing the day ruled by the planet with which I intend to work: Monday for the Moon, Tuesday for Mars, Wednesday for Mercury, Thursday for Jupiter, Friday for Venus, Saturday for Saturn, Sunday for the Sun. On those days the influence of the related planets is considered to be the highest. This can also be further emphasized by electing the hours ruled by the planets.

If, on the one hand, it can be important to consider the most suitable time (although it should never become an obsession), on the other it is essential to remember that the time to which I refer here is not merely conventional time. It is a sacred space produced by the melting of past, present and future. This can easily be misunderstood, as it does not have the usual applications in the ordinary perception of the world. Our habitual language structure – based on the net distinction of past, present and future tense, and of personal pronouns – seldom encourages an alternative awareness of time. Most shamanic languages do not have tenses to express past or future time in a linear sense. When an elder narrates the epic enterprises of heroes and gods, he does not talk about this as something that happened in the past, but rather he describes the process as something that continues to go on in the present or in another dimension to which he can choose to move at will. Time was created in such linear form as a way to justify fear. Here the content of painful experiences of the past are projected in to a future of which I am afraid, for it is unknown. Sacred time contains both past and future. It is indeed timeless. In order to access it I need to release the hold that conventional time has over my perception of life.

Non-ordinary Traits

The relationship with shamanic realities and the expression of related talents are experiences accessible to all human beings. In this regard, the examination of the natal chart allows the identification of factors that give clues about the individual's potentials. Some of these factors indicate a strong perception of unconventional states of consciousness that can become sources of instability when not understood or harmoniously employed.

Here we call such factors *non-ordinary traits*. The presence or lack of these factors has nothing to do with the level of maturity of the individuals concerned. The natal chart, in this as in all cases, describes a potential whose actual expression depends on the individual. The responsibility of those who possess non-ordinary traits is the same as for anyone: to become aware of one's Intent and connect it with the Function so as to release the illusion of separation. Non-ordinary traits includes *alien* and *mutant characters*.

The term *alien traits* was created by Edwin C. Steinbrecher[6] to identify, through the presence or absence of planets in specific astrological positions, highly specialised non-ordinary talents and abilities. This term is not used to indicate the extra-terrestrial provenance of an individual, but to define his subjective feelings regarding his nature and experience on Earth. A common characteristic of aliens consists in being aware of their powers until their first transit of Saturn squares their natal Saturn. This passage, which occurs around the age of seven, is a crucial time for everybody. It marks the relinquishment of perceptions which are incompatible with conventional reality. It also represents the beginning of the organisation of the defence system that allows life to be faced in the fiction of the consensus reality. The child, as he connects with the structures of ordinary education and customs, starts to learn the *cunning tricks* of this world and to become accustomed to the mask of his ego. This period of time seems to have extreme consequences for aliens. Sometimes they impose themselves on their friends, creating a veil of reverence, fear and mystery around themselves. They can also isolate themselves or behave in unusual ways so that they are considered weird or abnormal, and as a result they can receive either a social or self-inflicted ban. In both cases these individuals react to feelings that they are different from other people and then begin to build an ego based on a strong sense of alienation. In order to survive in the family and social environment, alien characters are often forced to suffocate their nature and non-ordinary capacities or to live them in total secrecy as if they were addictions or perversions. As their environment looks at such potentials as anomalies or a source of danger, those who have them also end up condemning them as negative.

During adolescence, and especially at the time of the transit of Saturn opposed Saturn (14–15 years) and the following Saturn square Saturn (21–22 years), alien characters can experience acute phases of depression with consequences that risk becoming fatal (accidents, suicides, addiction to drugs, etc.). A typical feature of aliens, as well as mutants, is usually that of experiencing strong traumas in the pre-natal time or in the first months of life. In order to outlive such wounds they tend to find refuge in non-ordinary dimensions. This causes their connections with those environments to open up exceptionally or prematurely. This also implies that, although they are apparently present on the ordinary dimension of this planet, their perceptions are not. It follows that they can easily experience themselves as living here as aliens. According to circumstances and the nature of their energetic connections, these individuals develop and transform in various ways. Alien and mutant characters of Neptune and Uranus, for example, generally have an early development of their higher chakras leading to the expression of excessive subtle frequencies (compared to those of the Earth) which reflect into strong limitation and dissatisfaction toward material life. In these instances, to balance such energies and express them as talents in ordinary life, they often need to open up to lower chakras and ground their energy into the Earth.

Alien traits consist of *powers, vessels, instruments* and *adepts*. The *alien powers* are those with the Sun in conjunction with Saturn, Uranus, Neptune or Pluto (allowing a 8° orb).[7] They have the capacity to *extend,* or *radiate,* their specific energy field into the physical plane, affecting and changing all they connect with. Their task is to bring awareness of other dimensions and states of perception (mainly related to Level 2). They have profound effects on others, whether or not they are conscious of their talents. 'They are like arrows of light and roaring thunderbolts that proudly storm in the somnolence of nocturnal darkness. Each in its way, proud and with no hesitation, breaks off and suspends the fragile hallucinations of mankind, levelling and indicating the way to those who in that moment are awake.'[8]

The *alien vessels* are born with Moon conjunct with Saturn, Uranus, Neptune or Pluto (allowing a 6° orb). They act *magnetically,* drawing their specialised energies toward themselves and the people they connect with. They work as *gates* to other dimensions (mainly related to Level 2) and are able to receive specific energies from others and return them as purified, heightened, and more conscious energy forms. Whether or not they are aware of their magnetic effect on others, they are operative. According to Ur Kuran their role is that of preserving and nourishing the development of non-ordinary potentials just as mothers take care of their children in the period before and after birth. 'Ignoring all possible dangers, they firmly lay the eggs of the worlds which exist beyond the human hallucinations. With care they brood them and nourish their embryo until it is ready to disclose and proceed autonomously. At any moment they remain totally available to nurture and protect the potentials of light they have generated.'[9]

The *alien instruments* have Saturn, Uranus, Neptune or Pluto in the first house of their chart or in conjunction with the Ascendant from the twelfth house (allowing an 4° orb). They operate as *amplifiers, receivers* and *broadcasters* of the energies they represent. Their capacities seem to be intrinsic to their physical bodies, so that they often possess unusual anatomical features.

In general, aliens 'have the ability to contain and to radiate energies which in a non-alien being would "blow the circuits" unless the body and the psyche had been trained and prepared to receive and radiate them. Sometimes the aliens have trouble with their abilities, which often frighten and disturb them – especially when these abilities awaken unexpectedly.'[10]

Another category of aliens, called the a*depts*, are those born with neither the Ascendant nor any planet in a particular quality (cardinal, fixed or mutable) or element (fire, earth, water, air). Far from being deprived of their missing quality or element, these people express them at their best, provided they are aware of their spiritual path. If this is not the case, such faculties are blocked, although they can be used or exploited by other people.

Mutant characters are those born with Saturn, Uranus, Chiron, Neptune or Pluto conjunct (with a 8° orb) to Immum Coeli (*mutant roots*) or Medium Coeli (*mutant flowers*). They identify qualities and inclinations that allow accelerated transformation of grievances and passage beyond the illusion of separation. Mutants have the possibility to cut a way in the spiral of their current existence and acquire a wider perception that can cause consistent changes both in their lives and those of the people and situations around them. According to the *Epic of the Sacred Cone* these people may play an important strategic role in the restructuring and reawakening of human multi-dimensional awareness.

Similarly to alien traits, mutant traits express in the individual concerned, whether he is aware of them or not. When the power coming from non-ordinary traits is not understood, accepted or employed according to an Intent connected to the Function, serious problems arise. Sometimes the original potential of these traits can be stimulated through significant relationships with individuals having similar patterns. Although the motivation of certain meetings appears to be different (friendship, work, sexual attraction, study, therapy, relationship, etc.), their actual purpose is that of correcting and stimulating the expression of non-ordinary traits. In order to develop these potentials, besides this process of activation through other individuals, it is necessary to ensure a precise commitment and take responsibility for one's power. This condition is enhanced by the relationship with the Spirit Guide and Paheka (Totem Spirit). In particular it is helpful to contact the Totem Spirit related to the non-ordinary trait and ask it, under the supervision of the Spirit Guide, to provide teachings. For this purpose specific tools can be employed in the form of parts of the body or sacred objects. Among the latter, in the Sacred Cone Circle, the *trevillan stones* are used. These are stones collected in ceremonial lands, on which seals related to alien or mutant characters are energetically carved.

Another category is that which Steinbrecher calls *protectors*. These are individuals who have no alien patterns in their chart. They seem to function in a protective and understanding way towards the aliens, balancing their moods, warning them when they get too weird or scary for other people, and acting as mediators or interpreters for them to others. 'They generally have not suffered the social rejection and alienation that the Aliens have experienced, and those people who have Alien patterns don't frighten the Protectors or make them nervous as they do others.'[11] As they have not experienced the early repression and distortion of non-ordinary traits that the Aliens have, Protectors can develop and refine such talents much more rapidly than the Aliens, especially when they have the chance to be close to the latter.

1 The term *twelve-letter alphabet,* also called *Zip Code,* was coined by the American astrologer and anthropologist Zipporah Pottenger Dobyns, and subsequently employed by her daughter, Maritha Pottenger, one of the main pioneers of experiential astrology. Among their works: Zipporah Pottenger Dobyns, *Finding the Person in the Horoscope,* ACS Publications, 1973; *Expanding Astrology's Universe,* TIA, 1983; Maritha Pottenger, *Complete Horoscope Interpretation: Putting Together your Planetary Profile,* ACS, 1986; *Encounter Astrology,* TIA, 1978.

2 Maritha Pottenger, *Complete Horoscope Interpretation: Putting Together Your Planetary Profile*, ACS, 1986, pp. 9–10.

3 Marcus Allen, *Astrology for the New Age: An Intuitive Approach*, CRCS Publications, 1979, p. 28.

4 Please find further information in the chapters related to the corresponding sectors – Sector 1 (Ascendant), Sector 4 (Immum Coeli), Sector 7 (Descendant), Sector 10 (Medium Coeli) – in the second book of this text.

5 See note 7 in Chapter 2.

6 For further information about this topic see: Edwin C. Steinbrecher, *The Inner Guide Meditation: A Spiritual Technology for the 21st Century*, Samuel Weiser, 1988.

7 The indication of the orb in brackets refer to my understanding, which also includes the awareness that the closer the orb the stronger the effect.

8 Notes from teachings by Ur Kuran.

9 Ibid.

10 Steinbrecher, *Inner Guide Meditation*, p. 225.

11 Ibid. p. 183.

APPENDIX

The Abridged Compendium of the Game of the Sacred Cone

Our pristine remembrances originate from a state of such an ecstasy and serenity, whose bliss no human words will ever manage to convey. Yet a parlance is to be applied herewith to articulate what is beyond all attainable languages. And so we proceed, repletely aware of the forlorn nature of our enterprise, with the narration of those events which generated the perception of this universe of space and time where we, on an endless search, appear to navigate.

In the *Sphere of Light*, in that immaculate and magnificent location that dwells beyond what is beyond, there is an environment which we promptly attempt to depict as a constellation and whose name is *Handor*. This unmentionable site and its inhabitants have a most peculiar characteristic. They are fond of games and consume their lives playing, dancing, chanting and celebrating all categories of affairs. Their idiom incorporates silences, songs, laughter, dance, stillness and other expressions which cannot obviously be translated into any human tongue. Besides that, there is another prominent idiosyncrasy which is distinctive of Handor. It is the *Last Frontier* of the Sphere of Light. What does the *Last Frontier* signify? Well, that is an elongated chronicle and, although it is an inconceivable and, alas, forlorn enterprise, we will endeavour to explain it in human terms.

One day, there on Handor, something unthinkable transpired. The Sphere of Light attained its *Peak*. It necessitated an interminable time to reach that Peak. For uncountable cycles of ages, the collective consciousness of Handor had exchanged light with the Centre of the Sphere. Then, the Peak was achieved and Handor could shine as a brimful emanation of light itself. The fact of having grown up to the maximum possible luminosity was an imposing accomplishment for the Sphere of Light. This brought such joy for the Handorians and a constant climax of ecstasy and luminosity which was so... Well, we give up any attempt to describe that! It is really too much and we risk blowing up our human circuits even if we only try to convey it in mere words.

After some time, together with this sense of indescribable ecstasy, the Handorians commenced to experience something unforeseen. The Peak had elected to continue peaking. His light needed to locate another direction to wend his way. Handor could not contain it anymore. But where could it proceed if Handor was the Last Frontier? This was the prevailing dilemma. The most conspicuous response at this stage seemed to be that of stretching beyond the Frontier. But for the Handorians that answer was not at all translucent. Nobody had ever ruminated on moving beyond the Last Frontier. And that was actually the reason why it was named the Last Frontier. To the farther side of it, there was nothing at all and one could not even conceive the idea of proceeding beyond. 'How can you journey to a place where nothing exists? How can you frolic in darkness? Why on Handor should we move farther? What's the point?' crooned most Handorians. On the one hand this sounded very reasonable, while on the other there were grounds to hold diverse points of view.

'That's the challenge of a novel game!' warbled a consortium of Handorians. 'We hold light; while there, beyond the Frontier, there is only darkness. Now, as a centre of light, we do need to come to terms with that darkness." For most Handorians these views did not make any sense. However this did not prevent them from spreading throughout Handor. After a short time the issue of darkness provided the idea for the unravelling of a revolutionary game. The theme was so riveting and controversial that this *Game* gradually became acutely renowned. Anon it disseminated in the whole constellation. It was called the *Game of the Sacred Cone* and, as time went on, it elaborated different variations. Appropriate arenas were erected to play it. There, thanks to a contrivance entitled the *Sacred Cone*, it was feasible to captivate and emit darkness. At a certain stage of the *Game*, often just for a few instants, the whole perimeter of the arena would sink into an unmitigated condition of obscurity. That was truly an unprecedented occurrence for the Handorians. In those exceptional circumstances they would convene in earnest immobility, amazement and taciturnity. Then, when the darkness was over, the Handorians could chortle at the weirdness of such an experience.

Darkness was extremely scarce on Handor and in all the Sphere of Light in general. In order to reproduce it, the mammoth conic reservoirs based in the directional stations of the constellation were employed. Before the introduction of the *Game,* most Handorians did not comprehend anything about those reservoirs or did not even know they existed. Nobody had ever been interested in darkness except for a minuscule bundle of eccentric researchers. The success of the *Game* caused an impetuous augmentation of solicitation for darkness. Soon the reservoirs risked running out of darkness. After some time the quantity of darkness was so pigmy that the Handorians were faced with a crucial decision: either to suspend the *Game* or consider the idea of moving where darkness was supposed to be abundant, i.e. beyond the Last Frontier. This latter option was still regarded as cretin and devoid of any sense. Rather than implementing it, most Handorians were ready to let go of the *Game of the Sacred Cone* and either return to their traditional games or devise something else. Yet a minority were extremely devoted to the *Sacred Cone* and would do whatever in order to preserve the *Game.* In their songs they invited immediate action as darkness was running short and this risked extinguishing their beloved *Game.* Then the Peak himself emerged in the Central Stadium of Hartem (the most resplendent of the twelve major stars of Handor) and chanted a hymn which sounded more or less like: 'Oh beloved ones, you have been training yourselves for aeons, and you already have your *Circle of Champions* in this *Game.* Now it's time to direct an elected team beyond the Last Frontier to play with real darkness. Your cones are vacant and if you intend to persist in the *Game,* you are to take a decision.' The *Circle of Champions,* who consisted of the major representatives of the Handorian Stars, were rather tumultuous at the news. 'And about time too!' they trolled. 'That's what we have been anticipating for ages!' The Peak was jocund at this attitude, but had to warn the Champions to be cautious about their choices: 'It's not going to be that smooth there. The *Game* is going to be different once you are in the darkness. You won't be able to turn on the light as you do in the arenas. Once you are beyond the Frontier everything is going to be very *serious* and you are likely to overlook that you are in the *Game* and you could even cease your songs and dances. Besides you would need a *spacesuit* whose way of functioning causes a lot to ponder on.' Of all the songs the Peak had ever sung this was really the most incomprehensible. '*Serious*? What does it signify? How is it possible to lose sight of the *Game*? How is it possible not to sing or dance?' chorused the Handorians. Now one should understand that Handorians did not have the word *serious* in their vocabulary. That word was really beyond their minds, as was also the fact of seeing life in a way different from games, songs and dances. The Peak had not finished though. There was a profound silence, as it was clear to everyone that the Peak was about to vocalise another major song. Then the Peak *said*: 'When you go beyond the Last Frontier, after a while you forget about the place where you come from and begin to feel as if you have been *abandoned*. You get *angry* with your original planet and as a form of *vengeance* you create a *separate* reality. Then you feel *guilty* about it and in order to escape from that *guilt* you create further *separation* and *vengeance* until the *pain* and the *boredom* is so unbearable that you sink into the Peak of the *Sphere of Darkness*. There you realise that you cannot move any further and you get so *fed up* that you are forced to recover your memory and original Intent. At that point you begin to undo all the reality you have been creating since the commencement of the *Game* until you come back to Handor.' All this was sheer gibberish for the Handorians. It was filled with words (see *italics*) which were a total mystery for them. Moreover, and what was really too much, this time the Peak did not sing nor dance. He *said* those words and this had never occurred before. Handorians were full of amazement. They did not comprehend what the Peak meant, but were at once aware that there was something mysterious about life which the Peak knew and they didn't. This created a lot of excitement among the Circle of Champions. 'We have never played anything like that. That's really a totally different game. We are going to bring light to the darkness! We are looking forward to going beyond the Last Frontier. Here we are, in readiness to go!' they sang.

The Champions unanimously accepted that they would depart and for such purpose initiated a long training in the star of Kallex by the homonymous Rock (i.e. the celebrated black *Rock of Kallex*). After many laborious and patient preparations and instructions, they were finally primed to leave Handor and move beyond the Last Frontier. They were called the *Pioneers of the*

Sacred Cone, as on the day of their departure the Peak addressed them as such. They consisted of the 12 best players of each of the 12 Handorian Stars (*Kirway, Kallex, Tudor, Ukar, Hanmar, Santjul, Friaan, Haxar, Vuolly, Trent, Framg, Hartem*), making a total of 144 Pioneers. The Peak said unto them: 'Beloved Pioneers, are you aware that it is your choice to play this game? That it is you who make the decision?' 'Of course!' chanted the Pioneers, 'What else could it be?' At which the Peak added: 'Are you aware that you are *united*?' According to Handorian standard awareness, this question did not make any sense, as the idea of separation was totally out of place in Handor. Nevertheless the Pioneers had received a training about separation and, although they still could not make up their mind about it, they had some vague theoretical idea regarding what the Peak had asked and therefore replied yes. 'Whatever happens,' said the Peak, 'Remember it is part of the *Game*. Always bear in mind the Basic Agreements of the *Game*. You are to reach the Peak of Darkness, sow the seeds of light of the *Sacred Cone,* fill the latter with darkness, and then return all together to Handor.'

The Pioneers departed with a fleet of twelve starships, one for each of the twelve stars of Handor. The starships cautiously descended into the abyss of the spiral leading beyond the Last Frontier. They soon found themselves in an incredibly void and lifeless area. The impact of such a dimension inspired chants and dances never performed before. After travelling for a long time, the Pioneers lost their bearings and the connection with Handor. This situation was part of the procedures of the *Game* and a very much expected development. Nevertheless it created considerable excitement and stupefaction. The Pioneers concluded that they were at the point half-way between Handor and the Peak of Darkness. According to the briefing received during the training, in that place, major key events for the Game would occur. After many songs and dances of reflection, the Pioneers elected to halt and build a base to be used as provisional point of reference until communication with Handor were re-established. During the lengthy works of construction of the base, spacesuits were worn for the first time. For the Pioneers it was rather unusual to sing and dance in those spacesuits. After a series of some rather awkward rhythms, the Pioneers managed to adjust to the spacesuits and create astonishing and fascinating melodies. They were called *Ur,* a term which was subsequently adopted as the denomination for the base. Once the works were concluded, the Pioneers planted some seeds of light from the

Sacred Cone to render the base visible after their departure. For this purpose a special glasshouse was fabricated. Out of those seeds astounding beings of light were born. They were called *Sadoha*. The birth of Sadoha was a major source of delight for all Pioneers. The bodies of those beings abounded in white light and ecstatic vibrations. After an extended period of training, the Sadoha were able to run Ur on their own. This allowed the Pioneers to set off again on their voyage toward the Peak of Darkness. Thanks to the light produced by Sadoha on Ur, the descent of the Handorian starships was reassuring. Although, as the Pioneers moved downward, the lights of Ur became weaker and weaker, their presence bestowed a sense of profound placidity and safeguard. Whenever they turned their awareness upward, the Pioneers could give ear to the ecstatic frequencies of the hymns of Sadoha and raise the energy required to face the obscure zones of their voyage.

After a tardy navigation, the Pioneers approached an area of extreme darkness. The obscurity was so condensed that the puissant headlights of the starships would not manage to produce any visibility. At first the Pioneers believed they had arrived at the Peak of Darkness. However, after a careful examination, they realised that they were indeed just drawing near to the point half-way between Handor and the Peak of Darkness. The major key events, mentioned so insistently during the training, were not only related to Ur, as it was conjectured. Most of them had still to occur. Something else was supposed to happen and the Pioneers did not have any clue. The lights of Ur were now dim far away in the sky. They resembled a few stitch-marks on a black cloth and to spot them required a considerable degree of attention. The Handorian starships connected with the Sadoha in Ur to check whether communication with Handor had been re-established. This was not the case though, and the Pioneers had to rely on Ur for hints on how to face the next development. The Sadoha suggested creating four additional bases around the area of darkness. The Pioneers decided to organise themselves into four fleets or *elements*, made up of three starships each, and to move horizontally instead of vertically, as they had done so far. Each element set off on a journey aimed at reaching the extreme point of their chosen direction, whose distance was determined in co-operation with Ur. Upon reaching their point, the Pioneers built a base and planted some seeds of light from the *Sacred Cone*. They also employed the spacesuits and, to their amazement, realised that the rhythms of the songs and dances had considerably changed. The fabric and the working of the spacesuit too had modified consistently. The four bases had noticeably specific characteristics and expressed the particular qualities of the spacesuit of their element. They were called *Ruha, Ratah, Rogah, Riallah*. Out of the seeds a new variety of Sadoha was generated. The bodies of those beings emitted a different light according to each base. Ruha was red, Ratah green, Rogah blue, and Riallah yellow. Also these Sadoha were trained until they were able to run the bases on their own. Finally, the four elements returned to the original point of darkness from which they had departed. After such a long time, they were most joyous to meet and reunite again. From that central point, which was called *Pahai*, they greatly rejoiced at their major achievements and triumphed in seeing the obscurity enlightened by the bright colours of the four directional bases, as well as by the dim white lights of Ur. The Pioneers were delighted at the sight of all that. It was the basic structure of a majestic cone with the apex in Ur, the directional points of the circle, or horizontal axis, in Ruha, Rata, Rogah, Riallah, and the centre in Pahai. Each element related such marvellous stories as regards the directional bases, the beings that populated them and their melodies. The Pioneers were stupefied by this and resolved to have a circular navigation around the horizontal axis to visit the four bases.

The journey around the horizontal axis and the visitation to the four directional bases was a most amazing enterprise which required a long cycle of time to be accomplished. Many songs and dances of a different quality were composed. Finally, the Pioneers reverted to the central point of Pahai. There they reconnected with the light of Ur and paused in order to decide upon further developments. During this time, the Pioneers commenced the witnessing of a series of eerie contretemps. According to the original instructions, such circumstances were part of the *Game*. The Pioneers understood that weird and crucial things would occur once they arrived in Pahai. However, what happened was indeed extremely outlandish and beyond any expectation. The construction of the directional bases had required an increased and constant use of spacesuits. This resulted in a growing interest in their functioning, maintenance and creative potentials. As a result some Pioneers experienced moments of failure of memory that caused them to forget essential details about Handor and the *Game*. They would also utilise their spacesuit in communication and produce new linguistic forms of expression. The most predominant of them consisted of *talking* and formulating *points of view* and *opinions* which gradually developed into *judgements* and *critiques*. Another aspect of these forms of communication is that they began to diverge consistently according to the elements involved. The Pioneers started to get some comprehension about the word *separation*. Among them two sides holding different views emerged. One part maintained that action was needed and light had to be sent so as to reach the Peak of Darkness, whereas the other part insisted on not taking any action and to hold the light in order to draw the Peak of Darkness. The contrast between these two sides came to be so acute that they decided to separate and to play the *Game* on their own. They organised themselves in two polarities made up of 6 starships and 72 Pioneers each. This split required a radical change in the structure and functioning of the starships and spacesuits.

At first the separation progressed like an eccentric joke. It looked like an exciting diversion aimed at stimulating the course of the *Game*. It was assumed that after some time the two parts would join again and abide by the basic agreements of the *Game*. Yet, as time went on, it became more and more strenuous to discern if the two sides were really willing to return to the original way of playing. The conflict intensified and this provoked the employment of queer and obdurate game strategies. A crucial clash occurred when each polarity started to construct two bases of secondary directions in the mid-point between one direction and the other. As a result the bases of *Ahur, Hatar, Hagor* and *Hallair* were settled. In those locations the *Seed of the Sacred Cone* was planted and new types of beings were born. They were called *Paheka*. Their bodies, so different from those of Sadoha, could generate both light and darkness.

The appearance of Paheka was a source of voluminous complacency for the Pioneers of each polarity. Darkness was a most recherché substance for Handorians. Following the success of the *Game of the Sacred Cone*, its value had become priceless. The 12 Paheka were able to produce darkness in almost unlimited quantities. This rendered them precious for the Pioneers just as diamond caves are for human beings. However, each Paheka would produce different dosages of darkness and light though. Such situations gradually determined a friction among Pioneers. Eventually that brought further separation. The original fleet was divided into 12 Sectors which represented the 12 Paheka and also the starships of the 12 stars of Handor. Each sector installed a base around the circumference of the great cone and began to work on its own. After ages of hostilities and combats, the sectors further separated themselves. In the end each of the 144 Pioneers decided to operate autonomously.

This separation into 144 single entities caused a major quandary, as the *Game*, in order to function effectively, required a minimum group of 12 united components. The Pioneers were forced to find a solution in order to assure the continuation of the *Game*. For this purpose they elected to utilise the Paheka. Each of the 144 Pioneers built a base and generated further Paheka. Each Pioneer began to be part of a circle made up of Paheka. As a result of this development the *Game* received a substantial impulse of creativity. The Paheka, however, were not beings of light, but of both light and darkness. As they were born after the process of separation, they were alien to the original thought form of unity. They would find it easier to work as couples, or polarities. They would also tend to produce situations of severe warfare or captivation within their polarities. In order to master the *Game*, each Pioneer had to bring considerable modifications to his spacesuit and also employ high quantities of energies in toiling strategic relationships with each of the Paheka. As long as the Pioneers managed to keep the command of this convoluted situation, the *Game* would run well. When this was not the case, stern inconveniences easily resulted. The cardinal one occurred when the Paheka realised that they could mate between themselves and generate a seed of their own without the assistance of the Pioneers. From this seed various forms of life were created. The Paheka began to use them to develop a new version of the *Game*. The Pioneers were gradually deserted by their Paheka and were unable to play the *Game* properly. In the meantime the Paheka created bases and expanded their dominion in the Sphere until, after a few ages, they assumed full control. The Pioneers decided to descend into the lands of the Paheka in the attempt to create alliances with their inhabitants. They began to relate with some of them and in particular with a group that we call here *Zruddha*. These were allured by the luminosity of the Pioneers and began to grant their services. The Pioneers managed to train and employ the Zruddha in the *Game*. This allowed them to retrieve some of their previous power. Yet there were major tribulations, for the Zruddha had a rather fragile and unstable nature. Their structures, moreover, after a period of time or under certain circumstances, would deteriorate and become totally useless. As a consequence the

Pioneers had to expend enormous amounts of energy to train more Zrudhha. The Paheka, on the other hand, once they came to be aware of the link between Pioneers and Zruddha, hardened the conditions of the latter. This further abated their duration. The Pioneers tried to devise various strategic operations but they all failed. In the end Pioneers and Paheka reached an agreement. The former agreed to confine themselves to their bases and acknowledged the dominion of Paheka over the vastness of the remaining territory of the Sphere. The Paheka, as an exchange, would provide the Pioneers with all the darkness they needed for the *Game*. The Pioneers, although they could only play in their bases, were excited by the unlimited quantities of darkness that they had at their disposal.

Since the commencement of their enterprise, the Pioneers' gestures were followed with much interest in the Handorian State System. Wide screens highlighted the arenas and prominently featured news about the expedition beyond the Last Frontier. Handorians were startled at what was occurring and when they received information regarding the confinement of the Pioneers to their bases, well, they really could not take anymore. They decided to call upon the Peak of Light and ask for explanations. Hence the Peak agreed to reveal a most arcane and staggering truth. 'All this severance that you have witnessed is not a novelty for me. There is a far more abundant portion of the *Game* of which I could not phrase any word. You would not have managed to understand. Now that you have followed the enterprises of the Pioneers, at last you can comprehend. Therefore I can finally relinquish my secret. Hang on to my utterance. Down there, beyond the Peak of Darkness, my beloved sister abides, together with her descendants and my devoted brothers. In a most archaic time we started a *Game*, the pristine edition of the *Game of the Sacred Cone*. Similarly we ended up separate from each other. Now the calling of our ancient union is bound to prevail. From my sister Rodnah, the Peak of Darkness, a Circle of Pioneers has left. They consist of twelve representatives for each state or Order of Rodnah (Yawrik, Xellak, Rodut, Raku, Ramnah, Lujtnas, Naairf, Raxah, Yllouv, Tnert, Gmarf, Metrah). In the midpoint of Pahai the Circle of Handor and Rodnah are destined to meet. This has not happened yet for the Pioneers of Rodnah behaved similarly to those of Handor. They first created a base called *Ru*. In that place they generated the counterparts of pure darkness of the Sadoha (Ma Sadoha). Then they separated themselves and began to produce grey counterparts with the dark matrix of the Paheka (Mare Paheka), The separation which you have witnessed occurred also in my times. Indeed I was part of the original group of the 144 Pioneers.'

Following this startling and unprecedented declaration, the Peak resolved to send a thirteenth starship directly from the central star of Handor. The thirteenth starship, composed of twelve Pioneers, first reached Ur and, with the assistance of the Sadoha, developed a planetary system called *Ur Handor.* Then, they descended through the vertical axis, landing at the central point of Pahai. Around that space spread the vast number of bases fabricated by the Pioneers and Paheka during myriads of ages. The thirteenth starship halted in the central point of Pahai waiting to establish contact with the thirteenth starship of the Pioneers coming from Rodnah. After a substantial amount of time the meeting took place. [...]

The modalities of this event are for the time being unmentionable. In the end, the two sides arranged their starships in parallel, one above the other, composing the first structure of the base called Pahai. From that site the thirteenth Pioneers of Handor were solicited to descend along the vertical axis to reach Ru Rodnah, the vertical planetary base of Rodnah. At the same time the Pioneers of Rodnah ascended to Ur Handor, the vertical planetary base of Handor. After depositing the 144 seals of the original Pioneers of each side, the thirteenth Pioneers returned altogether to Pahai. [...]

It is not possible to disclose the procedures of the settling of the seals even with a metaphor. [...]

Then the Pioneers of each side started the search for the original Pioneers. For this purpose they began to fabricate the base of Pahai and to cover its surface through the use of connecting entities called Bhi Jinah. [...]

The construction of Pahai and the retrieval of the original Pioneers is still in progress. Each of the components of the thirteenth starships has to retrieve and conduct to Pahai the twelve Pioneers of each of the twelve original starships. Once the original Pioneers have been retrieved, the Handorian starships will continue up to Ru, expanding in that direction the structure of Pahai. Similarly the starships of Rodnah will proceed towards Ur. Handor and Rodnah's starships are aimed at widening Pahai within the whole area of the Grey Sphere until they reach Rodnah and Handor respectively. This enterprise manifests through the germination of Bhi Jinah. [...]

In order to prevent this accomplishment the Paheka with matrix of light (*Hare Paheka*) copulated with those of matrix of darkness (*Mare Paheka*) and generated a huge web of block in the horizontal axis aimed at obstructing the work of the Pioneers. This web, called *Paheka Rubhe,* consists of the 144 binary relationships between Hare Paheka and Mare Paheka. These relationships gave birth to 144 beings called *Graha* who, as time went on, multiplied themselves and generated all the varieties of Graha who exist in the Grey Sphere. The presence of this web determined a situation of block and stagnation in the whole area of Pahai.

The original Pioneers have to complete the Game as agreed. In order to do that they have to release the Graha, the Paheka web and the Paheka themselves. This is possible only if they manage to find their original unity. This is attainable only if they succeed in reaching Rodnah together, move through Ru, and vice versa. This is possible, for indeed there are no other possibilities. [...]

BIBLIOGRAPHY

Achterberg, Jeanne, *Imagery in Healing: Shamanism and Modern Medicine*, New Science Library, Boston, MA, 1985.

Allen, Marcus, *Astrology for the New Age: An Intuitive Approach*, CRCS Publications, Sebastopol, CA, 1979.

Andrews, Ted, *Animal-Speak*, Llewellyn, St. Paul, MN, 1995; *Magickal Dance: Your Body as an Instrument of Power*, Llewellyn, St. Paul, MN, 1993.

Arrien, Angeles, *The Four-Fold Way: Walking the Paths of the Warrior, Teacher, Healer and Visionary*, Harper, San Francisco, CA, 1993.

Arroyo, Stephen, *Astrology, Karma and Transformation: The Inner Dimensions of the Birth Chart*, CRCS, Sebastopol, CA, 1992; *Astrology, Psychology and the Four Elements: An Energy Approach to Astrology and Its Use in the Counselling Arts*, CRCS, Sebastopol, CA, 1975.

Ashcroft-Novicki, Dolores, *The Ritual Magic Workbook: A Practical Course of Self-Initiation,* The Aquarian Press, Wellingborough, 1986.

Baigent, Michael and Richard Leigh, *The Elixir and the Stone: Unlocking the Ancient Mysteries of the Occult*, Penguin, London, 1998.

Baigent, Michael; Richard Leigh; Henry Lincoln, *The Holy Blood and the Holy Grail*, Arrow, London, 1996.

Baldwin, Christina, *Calling the Circle: The First and Future Culture*, Bantam Books, New York, NY, 1998.

Bloom, William, *Angels, Fairies and Nature Spirits*, Piatkus, London, 1998.

Boncompagni, Solas, *Il mondo dei simboli: numeri, lettere e figure geometriche,* Edizioni Mediterranee, Roma, 1984.

Bragdon, Emma, *A Sourcebook for Helping People in Spiritual Emergency*, Lightening Up Press, Los Altos, CA, 1988.

Bramley, William, *The Gods of Eden*, Avon Books, New York, NY, 1989.

Bryant, Page, *Starwalking: Shamanic Practices for Traveling into the Night Sky*, Bear & Company, Santa Fe, NM, 1997.

Caddy, Eileen, *Flight Into Freedom,* Findhorn Press, Findhorn, 2002; *God Spoke to Me*, Findhorn Press, Findhorn, 1971; *Opening Doors Within*, Findhorn Press, Findhorn, 1986; *The Spirit of Findhorn,* Findhorn Press, Findhorn, 1977.

Caddy, Peter, *In Perfect Timing: Memoirs of a Man for the New Millennium*, Findhorn Press, Findhorn, 1996.

Cahill, Sedona and Joshua Halpern, *The Ceremonial Circle: Practice, Ritual, and Renewal for Personal and Community Healing,* Harper, San Francisco, CA, 1992.

Campbell, Joseph, *The Hero with a Thousand Faces*, Princeton University Press, Princeton, NJ,1949.

Castaneda, Carlos, *A Separate Reality*, Simon and Schuster, New York, NY, 1971; *Tales of Power*, Simon and Schuster, New York, NY, 1974; *The Teachings of Don Juan: A Yaqui Way of Knowledge*, University of California Press, Berkeley, CA, 1968.

Cavendish, Richard, *The Black Arts*, Routledge & Kegan Paul, London, 1967.

Cerchio, Bruno, *Simbologia astrologica,* Edizioni Mediterranee, Roma, 1981.

Clifton, Chas S., *Witchcraft Today: Book Three, Witchcraft and Shamanism,* Llewellyn, St. Paul, MN, 1994.

Clow, Barbara Hand, *Liquid Light of Sex: Understanding Your Key Life Passages,* Bear & Company, Santa Fe, NM, 1991.

Conforto, Giuliana, *Man's Cosmic Game*, Edizioni Noesis, 1998. *La futura scienza di Giordano Bruno e la nascita dell'uomo nuovo*, Macro Edizioni, Diegaro di Cesena, 2001.

Cook, Angelique S. and G.A. Hawk, *Shamanism and the Esoteric Tradition,* Llewellyn, St. Paul, MN, 1992.

Cook, Roger, *The Tree of Life: Symbol of the Centre*, Thames and Hudson, London, 1974.

Cunningham, Donna, *An Astrological Guide to Self-Awareness,* CRCS Publications, Sebastopol, CA, 1978; *Astrology and Spiritual Development,* Cassandra Press, San Rafael, CA, 1989; *Astrology and Vibrational Healing,* Cassandra Press, San Rafael, CA, 1988; *Being a Lunar Type in a Solar World,* Samuel Weiser, York Beach, ME, 1982; *Healing Pluto Problems*, Samuel Weiser, York Beach, ME, 1986; *Moon Signs: The Key to Your Life,* Ballantine, New York, NY, 1988.

Davis-Wolfe, Mattie and David Thomson, *Walking the Sacred Wheel: A Year's Journey of Initiation around the Sacred Wheel,* Sacred Circles Institute, Mukilteo, WA, 1995.

De Solange, Mailly Nesle, *Astrology: History, Symbols and Signs*, Inner Traditions International, New York, NY, 1985.

Dobyns, Zipporah Pottenger, *Expanding Astrology's Universe,* ACS Publications, San Diego, CA, 1983; *Finding the Person in the Horoscope*, TIA Publications, Los Angeles, CA, 1973.

Drake, Michael, *The Shamanic Drum: A Guide to Sacred Drumming,* Talking Drum Publications, Goldendale, WA, 1991.

Drury, Nevill, *The Elements of Shamanism,* Longmead, Shaftesbury, 1982; *The Shaman and the Magician*, Routledge & Kegan Paul, London, 1978.

Eliade, Mircea, *Shamanism: Archaic Techniques of Ecstasy*, Princeton University Press, Princeton, NJ, 1972; *Yoga: Immortality and Freedom*, Princeton University Press, Princeton, NJ,1970.

Essene, Virginia and Irving Feurst, *Energy Blessings from the Stars: Seven Initiations*, S.E.E. Publishing Company, Santa Clara, CA, 1998.

Essene, Virginia and Sheldon Nidle, *You Are Becoming a Galactic Human*, S.E.E. Publishing Company, Santa Clara, CA, 1994.

Findhorn Community, *The Findhorn Garden*, Findhorn Press, Findhorn, 1988.

Foley Davidsson, Marcy, William L. Shaffer and Kent Davidsson, *Illuminating Physical Experience*, Holistic Wellness Foundation, Boulder, CO, 2000.

Foundation for Inner Peace, *A Course in Miracles*, Foundation for Inner Peace, Glen Ellen, CA, 1992; *Psychotherapy; Purpose, Process, and Practice: An Extension of the Principles of A Course in Miracles,* Foundation for Inner Peace, Mill Valley, CA, 1976.

Frazer, James George, *The Golden Bough: The Roots of Religion and Folklore*, Avenel Books, New York, NY, 1981.

Gardner, Laurence, *Bloodline of the Holy Grail*, Element, Shaftesbury, 1996; *Genesis of the Grail Kings: the Pendragon Legacy of Adam and Eve*, Bantam, New York, NY, 1999.

Gawain, Shakti, *Creative Visualization*, Bantam, New York, NY, 1982.

Giamario, Daniel and Carolyn Brent, *The Shamanic Astrology Handbook*, JCAU Publications, Tucson, AZ, 2002.

Gilchrist, Cherry, *Planetary Symbolism in Astrology*, Saros Foundation, 1980.

Goodman, Felicitas D., *Speaking in Tongues: A Cross-Cultural Study of Glossolalia*, University of Chicago Press, Chicago, IL, 1972; *Where the Spirits Ride the Wind: Trance Journeys and Other Ecstatic Experiences*, Indiana University Press, Bloomington, IN, 1990.

Gore, Belinda, *Ecstatic Body Postures: An Alternate Reality Workbook*, Bear & Company, Santa Fe, NM, 1995.

Grof, Christina and Stanislav Grof, *The Stormy Search for the Self: A Guide to Personal Growth through Transformational Crisis*, Jeremy Tracher, New York, NY, 1990.

Guttman, Ariel and Kenneth Johnson, *Mythic Astrology: Archetypal Powers in the Horoscope*, Llewellyn, St. Paul, MN, 1996.

Halifax, Joan, *Shamanic Voices: A Survey of Visionary Narratives*, E.P. Dutton, New York, NY, 1979.

Hand, Robert, *Horoscope Symbols*, Whitford Press, West Chester, PA, 1981; *Planets in Transits*, Para Research, Rockport, MA, 1976.

Haram, *Manuale laico di astrologia*, Savelli, Milano, 1979.

Harner, Michael, *The Way of the Shaman*, Harper, San Francisco, CA,1990.

Hess, Helene, *The Zodiac Explorer's Handbook: A Unique Guide to Using Your Birth Chart for Inner Exploration*, The Aquarian Press, Wellingborough, 1986.

Hesse, Hermann, *Narcissus and Goldmund*, Bantam Books, New York, NY, 1971; *Siddharta*, Bantam Books, New York, NY, 1971; *Steppenwolf*, Henry Holt, New York, NY, 1990.

Hoffman, Kay, *The Trance Workbook: Understanding and Using the Power of Altered States*, Sterling Publishing, New York, NY, 1998.

Horn, Arthur David, (with Lynette Anne Mallory-Horn), *Humanity's Extraterrestrial Origins: ET Influences on Humankind's Biological and Culural Evolution*, Silberschnur, Lake Montezuma, AZ, 1994.

Huxley, Aldous, *Brave New World*, Triad/Panther Books, St Albans, 1977; *Island*, Penguin Books, Harmondsworth, 1974.

Ingerman, Sandra, *Soul Retrieval: Mending the Fragmented Self*, Harper, San Francisco, CA, 1991.

Jenkins, Palden, *Living in Time: Learning to Experience Astrology in Your Life*, Gateway Books, Bath, 1987.

Jones, Prudence (ed.), *Creative Astrology: Experiential Understanding of the Horoscope*, The Aquarian Press, London, 1991.

Judith, Anodea, *Wheels of Life: A User's Guide to the Chakra System,* Llewellyn, St. Paul, MN, 1987.

Jung, Carl Gustav, *Collected Works of C.G. Jung: Vol. 13, Alchemical Studies,* Princeton University Press, Princeton, NJ, 1967; *Man and His Symbols,* Doubleday, Garden City, NY, 1964; *Memories, Dreams, Reflections,* Fontana Press, London, 1995.

Kingsley, Peter, *In the Dark Places of Wisdom,* Element, Shaftesbury, 1999.

Lamparelli, Claudio, *Tecniche della meditazione orientale,* Mondadori, Milano, 1985.

Lapassade, Georges, *Dallo sciamano al raver: saggio sulla transe,* Urra, Milano, 1997.

Lemesurier, Peter, *The Healing of the Gods: The Magic of Symbols and the Practice of Theotherapy,* Element Books, Longmead, 1988.

MacLean, Dorothy, *To Hear the Angels Sing: An Odyssey of Co-creation with the Devil Kingdom,* Findhorn Press, Findhorn, 1980.

Marciniak, Barbara, *Bringers of the Dawn: Teachings from the Pleiadans,* Bear & Company, Santa Fe, NM, 1992; *Family of Light,* Bear & Company, Santa Fe, NM, 1998.

Matthews, John, *The Celtic Shaman: A Handbook,* Element, Rockport, MA, 1992.

Matthews, Caitlin and John Matthews, *The Western Way: A Practical Guide to the Western Mystery Tradition,* Arkana, London, 1985.

Mayo, Jeff, *The Planets and Human Behavior,* CRCS Publications, Sebastopol, CA, 1985.

McKenna, Terence, *Food of the Gods: The Search for the Original Tree of Knowledge,* Rider, London, 1992.

McEvers, Joan (ed.), *Spiritual, Metaphysical and New Trends in Modern Astrology,* Llewellyn, St. Paul, MN, 1988.

Meadows, Kenneth, *Earth Medicine: A Shamanic Way to Self Discovery,* Element, Shaftesbury, Dorset, 1991.

Mendoza, Ramon G., *The Acentric Labyrinth: Giordano Bruno's Prelude to Contemporary Cosmology,* Element, Shaftesbury, 1995.

Merriman, Raymond, *Evolutionary Astrology: The Journey of the Soul Through States of Consciousness,* Seek-It Publications, Bloomfield, MI, 1991.

Mindell, Arnold, *The Shaman's Body: A New Shamanism for Transforming Health, Relationships, and the Community,* Harper, San Francisco, CA, 1993.

Mission Control and Zoe Jho, *E.T. 101: The Cosmic Instruction Manual for Planetary Evolution,* Thorsons, London, 1995.

Mundy, John, *Listening to Your Inner Guide,* Crossroad, New York, NY, 1995.

Myers, Robert 'Buz', *The Moon as a Trigger for Transformation,* RKM (audiocassette).

Natale, Frank, *Trance Dance: The Dance of Life,* Element, Shaftesbury, 1995.

Nevin, Bruce, *Astrology Inside Out: A New Approach to Astrology,* Para Research, Rockport, MA, 1982.

Nicholson, Shirley (ed.), *Shamanism: an Expanded View of Reality*, Theosophical Publishing House, Wheaton, IL, 1987.

Noble, Vicki, *Shakti Woman: Feeling Our Fire, Healing Our World,* Harper, San Francisco, CA, 1991.

Osho, *Hidden Mysteries*, Rebel Publishing House, Pune, 1997; *Meditation: The First and Last Freedom,* St. Martin's Press, New York, NY, 1996; *Tantra, Spirituality and Sex*, Rebel Publishing House, Pune, 1994; *Vigyan Bhairav Tantra, The Book of Secrets: A New Commentary*, Rebel Publishing House, Pune, 1991.

Picard, Eudes, *Astrologie Judiciare*, Leymarié, Paris, 1936.

Pottenger, Maritha, *Astro Essentials: Planets in Signs, Houses & Aspects,* ACS Publications, San Diego, CA, 1991; *Encounter Astrology*, TIA Publications, Los Angeles, CA, 1978; *Healing with the Horoscope: A Guide to Counselling,* ACS Publications, San Diego, CA, 1982.

Pratesi, Aniela, *Iniziazione all'astrologia evolutiva: il cammino dell'anima attraverso la carta natale*, Edizioni Mediterranee, Roma, 2002.

Reinhart, Melanie, *Chiron and the Healing Journey: An Astrological and Psychological Perspective*, Penguin, London, 1989.

Ridall, Kathryin, *Channeling: How To Reach Out To Your Spirit Guide*, Bantam, New York, NY, 1990.

River, Lindsay and Sally Gillespie, *The Knot of Time: Astrology and Female Experience*, The Women's Press, London, 1987.

Rose, Christina, *Astrological Counselling: A Basic Guide to Astrological Themes in Person to Person Relationships*, The Aquarian Press, Wellingborough, 1982.

Roth, Gabrielle, *Maps to Ecstasy: Teachings of an Urban Shaman,* Mandala, London, 1990.

Rudhyar, Dane, *Astrology and the Modern Psyche: An Astrologer looks at Depth-Psychology*, CRCS, Sebastopol, CA, 1976.

Rutherford, Leo, *The Book of Games and Warm Ups for Group Leaders,* Gale Centre, Loughton, 1994; *Principles of Shamanism*, Thorsons, London, 1996.

Sanchez, Victor, *The Teachings of Don Carlos: Practical Applications of the Works of Carlos Castaneda,* Bear and Co., Santa Fe, NM, 1995.

Sargent, Denny, *Global Ritualism: Myth & Magic Around The World,* Llewellyn, St. Paul, MN, 1994.

Santoro, Franco, *Iniziazione all'astrosciamanesimo: la via zodiacale alla Guida Interiore,* Edizioni Mediterranee, Roma, 2000; *Introduzione agli aforismi provvisori della rete binaria del Sacro Cono*, Sacred Cone Press, Bologna, 2000; *Provisoria*, Forlorn Press, Bologna, 1984; *A Provisional Guide Book to the First Level of the Operative Training in Astroshamanism*, Sacred Cone Press, Forres, 2001; (ed.) *ProvOrdo Etnai Sagdhanatabe*, Anaghaseva, Bologna, 1988.

Schermer, Barbara, *Astrology Alive!: Experiential Astrology, Astrodrama and the Healing Arts*, The Aquarian Press, Wellingborough, 1989.

Shone, Ronald, *Creative Visualization,* Thorsons, London, 1984.

Sicuteri, Roberto, *Astrologia e mito: simboli e miti dello Zodiaco nella Psicologia del Profondo,* Astrolabio, Roma, 1978.

Sitchin, Zecharia, *Divine Encounters: A Guide to Visions, Angels, and Other Emissaries*, Avon Books, New York, NY, 1995; *The Stairway to Heaven*, Avon Books, New York, NY, 1980; *The Twelfth Planet*, Avon Books, New York, NY, 1976.

Somé, Malidoma Patrice, *Of Water and the Spirit: Ritual, Magic, and Initiation in the Life of an African Shaman,* Penguin, New York, NY, 1994.

Small Wright, Machaelle, *MAP: The Co-creative White Brotherhood Medical Assistance Program*, Perelandra, Jeffersonton, VA, 1994.

Starhawk, *The Spiral Dance: A Rebirth of the Ancient Religion of the Great Goddess,* Harper, San Francisco, CA, 1989.

Steinbrecher, Edwin C., *The Inner Guide Meditation: A Spiritual Technology for the 21st Century,* Samuel Weiser, York Beach, ME, 1988.

Stevenson, Sandy, *The Awakener the Time is Now: You Can Fulfil Your Part in Earth's True Destiny,* Gateway Books, Bath, 1997.

Storm, Hyemeyohsts, *Seven Arrows*, Ballantine, New York, NY, 1972.

Sun Bear, Wabun Wind and Crysalis Mulligan, *Dancing With The Wheel: The Medicine Wheel Workbook,* Simon & Schuster, London, 1991.

Szanto, Gregory, *Astrotherapy: Astrology and the Realization of the Self,* Arkana, London, 1987.

Ten Dam, Hans, *Exploring Reincarnation,* Arkana, London, 1990.

Vitebsky, Piers, *The Shaman: Voyages of the Soul, Trance, Ecstasy and Healing from Siberia to the Amazon,* DBP, London, 1995.

Volguine, Alexandre, *L'esoterismo dell'astrologia,* Xenia, Milano, 1996.

Wapnick, Kenneth, *Forgiveness and Jesus: The Meeting Place of A Course in Miracles and Christianity,* Foundation for A Course in Miracles, Roscoe, NY, 1983; *Glossary-Index for A Course in Miracles,* Foundation for A Course in Miracles, Roscoe, NY, 1982.

Wapnick, Gloria and Kenneth Wapnick, *The Most Commonly Asked Questions About A Course in Miracles,* Foundation for A Course in Miracles, Roscoe, NY, 1995.

Watson, Donald, *A Dictionary of Mind and Spirit,* Deutsch, London, 1991.

Watts, Alan, *Psychotherapy East and West*, Pantheon, New York, NY, 1962; *The Way of Zen,* Pantheon, New York, NY, 1958; *The Wisdom of Insecurity,* Pantheon, New York, NY, 1951.

Weiner, Errol, *Transpersonal Astrology: Finding the Soul's Purpose,* Element, Shaftesbury, 1991.

Williamson, Marianne, *A Return to Love: Reflections on the Principles of A Course in Miracles,* HarperCollins, New York, NY, 1996.

Woolger, Roger, *Other Lives, Other Selves: A Jungian Psychotherapist Discovers Past Lives,* Doubleday, New York, NY, 1987.

Wosien, Maria-Gabriele, *Sacred Dance: Encounter with the Gods,* Thames and Hudson, London, 1974.

Zimmerman, Jack, in collaboration with Virginia Coyle, *The Way of Council,* Bramble Books, Las Vegas, NV, 1996.

© Drawing by Rachel Hemming Bray

ABOUT THE AUTHOR

Franco Santoro is a shamanic facilitator, experiential astrologer, member of the Findhorn Foundation, the developer of astroshamanism and supply director of the *Sacred Cone Circle*. In 1964 he started regular connections with non-ordinary dimensions that led him to live a parallel life which was often the cause of conflict in his relationship with conventional reality. In 1976, during a vision quest in Northern Scotland, he had a transformational experience which, after years of practice with shamans and medicine people, allowed him to find clarity about his connections and acknowledge his function as bridge between dimensions. His path of apprenticeship encompassed both the archaic traditions of his Italian natal descent and those of other adopted lineages. Since 1996 he has run the *Operative Training in Astroshamanism*, an intensive programme for shamanic practitioners and healers. He is the author of *A Guide Book to Astroshamanism,* Sacred Cone Press, 2001; *Astroshamanism: A Journey into the Inner Universe,* Findhorn Press, 2003; *Astroshamanism: The Voyage Through the Zodiac,* Findhorn Press, 2003, *Iniziazione all'astrosciamanesimo: la via zodiacale alla Guida Interiore,* Edizioni Mediterranee, 2000, (in Italian) and other works on related topics. He has also composed and produced a series of recordings, such as *Drumming for the Astroshamanic Voyage.*

Franco lives in Scotland, where he currently serves in the education area of the Findhorn Foundation and regularly runs workshops on astroshamanism and core programmes. If you would like to write to the author or receive information about his programmes, the address is: Franco Santoro, Cluny Hill College, Forres, Scotland IV36 2RD. Tel. +44 (0)1309 672288. Email: info@astroshamanism.org Website: www.astroshamanism.org

Thank you for your interest.

be sure to continue your exploration with

ASTROSHAMANISM

book 2

The Voyage through the Zodiac

by Franco Santoro

isbn 1-84409-013-2 (pub. autumn 2003)

FINDHORN Press

Findhorn Press is a publishing business of the Findhorn Community which has grown around the Findhorn Foundation in northern Scotland.

For further information about the Findhorn Foundation and the Findhorn Community, please contact:

Findhorn Foundation

The Visitors Centre
The Park, Findhorn IV36 3TY, Scotland, UK
tel 01309 690311 • fax 01309 691301
email vcentre@findhorn.org
www.findhorn.org

For a complete Findhorn Press catalogue, please contact:

Findhorn Press

305a The Park, Findhorn

Forres IV36 3TE
Scotland, UK
Tel 01309 690582
freephone 0800-389-9395
Fax 01309 690036

If you live in the USA or Canada, please send your request to:

Findhorn Press

c/o Lantern Books
One Union Square West, Suite 201
New York, NY 10003-3303

Wherever you live, you can consult our catalogue online at

findhornpress.com

and email us at

info@findhornpress.com